"Drew writes with vulnerability and [...] their own journey of self-discovery and [...]
—Nick Vujicic, New York Times best-selling author and world-renowned motivational speaker

"Motivation is easy to understand and feel temporary, but it's another thing to keep consistent and relevant on a daily basis. This book does both of those things while being challenging and prescriptive. Drew identifies the obstacles we all face, explains why they exist, and provides the solutions we need to create a more meaningful life. If you're wanting to really live and not just exist, read this book."
—Clint Pulver, Emmy Award-Winning Keynote Speaker and Author of *I Love It Here*

"What happens when, in a moment, the hopes and dreams you've had for your life seem to suddenly shatter? If you're like me, you appreciate being reminded about principles of truth that should be guiding forces in our lives. In *Stand Guard at the Door of Your Mind*, Drew Young nails it for people who desire to create a positive mindset, increase happiness, and achieve success. Drew writes with openness and authenticity about how his personal journey of anxiety, depression, years of being bullied, and even an attempted suicide led to life-changing enlightenment and understanding of truths he now shares with all of us!"
—Becky Mackintosh, Speaker and Bestselling Author of *Love Boldly*

"Drew Young has written a must-read classic for anyone who struggles with their thinking and wants to create a better life for themselves. Read this book—and learn from one of the best!"
—Todd Sylvester, President, Todd Sylvester Inspires, Beliefcast Show, Author and Mentor

"Do you want a proven method for personal success? Then plant mental seeds of progress, maintain constant vigilance, love the person you are growing into, and reap the bounties in the fall. And read Drew Young's book, *Stand Guard at the Door of Your Mind*, to become a masterful personal gardener of your mind.

"The lasting principles offered in this book can expand your consciousness and raise your level of responsibility and performance. Reminiscent of

John C. Maxwell's timeless leadership precepts, Young promotes appreciation, service, and magnet-strength goals that pull you in the right direction—the direction you design for personal happiness."

—Jodi Orgill Brown, Professional Speaker, Coach, and Bestselling Author of *The Sun Still Shines*

"*Stand Guard at the Door of Your Mind* will infuse you with the courage to break through the limits that have held you back. Reading Drew's life experience as an aspiring author who finally wrote the book, challenges to get in the college of his choice, and finally making his dreams happen, battling lifelong struggles and overcoming them, will inspire you to also see the power of success within yourself, and that failing is only failure if you give up. This book keeps the promise of tactical suggestions and ideas to live your best life, mixed between Drew's experience and the lessons of great speakers and authors of generations past. I recommend it!"

—Jason Hewlett, CSP, CPAE, Author of *The Promise to the One*, Speaker Hall of Fame

"Everyone needs to read this message. Drew's honesty, vulnerability, and hope will instill in the reader a drive and motivation to keep getting back up when they fall, overcome their challenges, and focus on progress over perfection."

—Richard Ostler, Host of the *Listen, Learn & Love* podcast and Bestselling Author of *Listen Learn & Love*

"Drew Young's new book invites us to take to heart God's promise, 'for the power is in them.' The most powerful choice we can make is to determine the character of the person we want to become. This book builds on the work of James Allen ("As a Man Thinketh") and others, in a way that applies enduring principles to the world of today, to the experiences and aspirations of those who will become the leaders of families, communities, businesses, and churches. Its pages express a profound faith that all things can work to our good if we are willing to put forth effort, faith, patience, and practice."

—Tom Christofferson, author of *A Better Heart: The Impact of Christ's Pure Love* and *That We May Be One: A Gay Mormon's Perspective on Faith and Family*

"Mindset matters! This vulnerable and insightful book highlights the importance of cultivating and protecting our greatest asset—our mind. Drew's words will add hope, encouragement, and direction as you strive to create a life of greater fulfillment for yourself and those you love."

—Dorie Clark, author of *Reinventing You*,

#1 communication coach in the world

—Marshall Goldsmith, Leading Global Coaches Awards and executive education faculty, Duke University Fuqua School of Business

"It is not about being perfect. It is about continuing to progress with hope, discipline, and kindness. How do I know that? Read Drew Young's terrific book and find out."

—Stephen M. R. Covey, The New York Times and #1 Wall Street Journal bestselling author of *The Speed of Trust*

STAND GUARD AT THE DOOR OF YOUR MIND

—————— *Dedication* ——————

To all those who have fallen down 1,000 times and think they're failures. What matters isn't how many times we fall, but how many times we get back up. This is for you.

STAND GUARD
AT THE DOOR OF
YOUR MIND

Drew Young

CFI

AN IMPRINT OF CEDAR FORT, INC.

SPRINGVILLE, UTAH

ISBN 13: 978-1-4621-3964-4

Published by CFI, an imprint of Cedar Fort, Inc.
2373 W. 700 S., Springville, UT 84663
Distributed by Cedar Fort, Inc., www.cedarfort.com

Library of Congress Control Number: 2021933191

Cover design by Courtney Proby
Cover design © 2021 by Cedar Fort, Inc.

Printed in the United States of America

10 9 8 7 6 5 4 3 2 1

Printed on acid-free paper

Table of CONTENTS

IT ALL STARTS
WITH A THOUGHT

The world-renowned poet, writer, and researcher Ralph Waldo Emerson once penned the phrase, "Great [individuals] are they who see that spiritual is stronger than any material force—that thoughts rule the world" (Emerson, n.d.).

Why are thoughts so important? Because they shape not only the way we see the world but who we become in the world.

If you had asked me when I was a teenager what I thought about thinking, I would've looked at you like you were funny. "Thinking? Why would I spend my time thinking? I'd rather play basketball or video games. Thinking requires too much effort and doesn't get me anywhere worth going."

Little did I know then, but it turns out that life is exactly what our thoughts make it, regardless of whether we are twelve, twenty-two, forty-two, or seventy-two.

Consider this architectural metaphor. If you were to ask a building designer what one of the most important first steps is in constructing a state-of-the-art structure, what do you think they would say? Lay a solid foundation. A solid foundation guarantees two things: first, safety and security when storms and calamities strike; and second, confidence and peace knowing that the structure will be able to stand strong and beautiful throughout its existence.

Similarly, thoughts are the metaphorical foundation of our lives. They shape everything we do. They can lead to lives filled with safety, security, confidence, and peace . . . or they can produce the opposite. When we determine to think positive, healthy, and virtuous thoughts, we will begin to live positive, healthy, and virtuous lives. The opposite is true, as well. When we think negative, unhealthy, immoral thoughts (which is easier to do), we will live negative, unhealthy, immoral lives.

When I was fourteen years old, I was sitting in a meeting at my church. I can't remember the speaker's name, but I remember she was a famous skier. She told us a story of how she got injured one day as she was trying out for the Olympic ski team. Her leg was severely broken, and the doctors told her that she would be out of skis indefinitely. This was a very difficult time in her life, as she had to learn how to train her mind to not give up amidst a debilitating physical injury. She had to decide to either wallow in self-pity and discouragement, or choose to think positively and try and make the best of her situation. Day in and day out she battled negative thoughts that tried to destroy her self-confidence and her self-worth. Day in and day out she had to make a deliberate choice to control her thoughts so that her actions would be those of strength and courage. She relayed to us how every day she would take twenty minutes and just think. She would think about her situation and where she would be a year later as a result of her full recovery. She put pictures on her walls of Olympic skiers and vowed that she would achieve that goal. She trained, meditated, and trained some more.

When a thought of fear or distress tried to make its way into her mind, she pushed it away by saying, "I am going to make it! I am not giving up! I am responsible for my future!"

A year after her accident she tried out again for the US ski team and made it. Her experience taught her a great lesson: our life is what our thoughts make it, and we become what we think about most frequently.

She finished her speech by saying something that I remember to this day, and I hope it will help you in your life: "The longer you think about something, the more likely you are to do it" (n.a., personal communication, 2010).

Now, she wasn't talking about *over-thinking* something (obviously the more you do that, the less likely you are to do it), but rather focusing on something specific. The longer we think of things that are immoral, pornographic, violent, or crude, the more likely we are to engage in those acts. The longer we think of things that are virtuous, kind, powerful, inspirational, and confidence-building, the more likely we are to engage in those acts.

(A quick side note to those reading this that have mental or emotional illness or disabilities: your situation may be different, and it may not be possible to just think positively and never have a rough day. I feel for you. I've experienced those same feelings in my own battle with anxiety and depression. Things will improve with time as you accept help, utilize professional resources, and keep trying. Don't give up.)

The ball is in our courts. We are in charge of our minds, so we are in charge of our lives. We are responsible for our thoughts, so we are responsible for our actions and ultimately who we become. This doesn't mean that we'll never fall prey to temptation or negative thoughts. We're all human, and failing is part of life. What it does mean is that we can learn together to better control our minds and shape our futures in the best way possible.

One final thought: throughout this book you'll notice that I talk a lot about creating a better life or, in other words, how to use foundational principles and techniques to increase your chances of fulfillment and happiness throughout your life. Now, you may ask yourself two questions: 1) Why would you name this book *Stand Guard at the Door of Your Mind* if you're talking about creating a better life? That makes me think it's a book about mind control. 2) What does a twenty-five-year-old kid know about creating a better life? He has barely started adulthood and hasn't even *experienced* what life is yet.

Allow me to address these two questions:

First, this book is titled *Stand Guard at the Door of Your Mind* because everything we've ever created in our lives—everything around us, everything that will ever come into existence until the end of time—started with a thought. Every result that has ever been attained, whether evil or incredible, began with someone thinking about it beforehand.

Do you think Adolph Hitler decided one morning to get up and annihilate an entire civilization of Jewish people? Do you think that Mother Teresa walked outside one afternoon and just suddenly began helping the sick and afflicted? Do you think Michael Jordan decided one day that he was going to be on the Chicago Bulls, so he went to their practice facility and they welcomed him onto the team without any try-out whatsoever?

No. Everything started with a thought. Everything started with an idea to create a life-changing result. So yes, in terms of creating a better life, and achieving results that are fulfilling and remarkable, we need to start by standing guard at the door of our minds.

3

Second, you're right. I'm twenty-five years old. But you know what? I've gained experience and have gone through things that most people can't even comprehend in their thirties or forties (excuse the humble brag). I am a student, a writer, a reader, a listener, and a worker. I've read or listened to more than 100 books since I graduated high school on topics ranging from depression to business strategy to mindset to communication (don't believe me, ask my wife). I have listened to hundreds of audio recordings of some of the greatest motivational speeches of all time given by Jim Rohn, Les Brown, Zig Ziglar, Earl Nightingale, Margaret Thatcher, Winston Churchill, Rosa Parks, Mother Teresa, and dozens more. I professionally published my first book/memoir at the age of twenty-four after five years of writing and rewriting, editing and re-editing, and rejection after rejection. I've been through the depths of depression and anxiety, experiencing nights of sheer darkness and panic, not knowing if I could make it to the next morning. I've contemplated suicide, attempted self-harm, and wept for hours on end due to my fractured emotional skeleton. I've been to years of therapy and taken countless medications to try and refill the emotional and mental crater in my mind. I've traveled the world experiencing different cultures and individuals who have taught and inspired me to be better. Last, I have tried and FAILED more times than I can count—so I know exactly what it's like to struggle, fall short, but rise above life's challenges.

Yes, I do believe that I have learned firsthand from my own experiences and those much wiser than me (more important) what it means to create a better life for you and for those you love. No, I'm not perfect, but I've tried to learn and grow just like you. So let's grow together and discover the beauty of our existence and the purpose of our creation.

Chapter 1

A BETTER LIFE

Marcus Aurelius was a Roman emperor from 161 AD to 180 AD. He was known as the last of the Five Good Emperors. Without a doubt, he was one of the greatest philosophical minds this world has ever known, and many of his words have forever been immortalized in the writing of his book *Meditations*. He wisely said, "The happiness of your life depends upon the quality of your thoughts" (Aurelius, n.d.).

Human beings are unique. We are unlike any other creature on earth. We not only can do things other lifeforms cannot, but one thing sets us apart from everything else as well: we have been given the dignity of choice. No other life-form on this planet has been given the amazing gift of choice—they are subject to instinct and the genetic code.

What would happen if you told a goose to fly west for the winter? It would ignore you. Which way would it fly? South. Why? Because that's where it has been genetically programmed to go. Human beings are different. We can go wherever we want to go. We can see whatever we want to see. We can be whoever we want to be. We can do all these things because we have the dignity of choice, and the dignity of choice comes from our ability to think.

If we don't like who we are or who we're becoming, we can choose to change. If we don't like our friend group, we can change it. If we don't like how we're being treated in a certain relationship, we can change it. We're not trees. We're not meant to go through life being acted upon instead of acting for ourselves.

Remember this: life doesn't get better by chance; it gets better by change.

How do we create a better life? We remember two things. First, we are in control of our thoughts, which means we are in control of ourselves. Second, if something isn't right in our lives, we have the power (and the responsibility) to change it.

One may say to this, "That's all very fine and good, but life doesn't just depend on thoughts. We can't just go around hoping things will get better. And I try to have happy thoughts all the time, but I still feel like my life is hard and difficult at times. Explain that one to me. You've just said that our thoughts determine our lives, but even though my thoughts are good, my life is hard."

To answer that more clearly, let's say we're farmers. We've been diligent and determined throughout the spring and summer months to plant, irrigate, and harvest a good crop. We've been up before the sun has risen, and we've gone to bed after the moon has made its place in its nightly orbit. We've hoped and worked and scrimped and saved to put food on the table for our family, sacrificing our wants for the betterment of those we love, and we realize that in the morning our crop will be ready to be harvested.

We walk outside the morning of the harvest to behold a sight that we have only dreamed of. The stalks are high, and the grain is flowing through the fields. We rally up workers and start reaping the work we've put in. We manage to collect one-fourth of our grains before the day is out.

That night, however, as we sleep peacefully in our beds, a giant hailstorm comes and beats the rest of our crop into the ground, destroying the remainder of the potential harvest. What do we do? Was all that work for nothing? Was all the planning, and saving, and tilling, and gardening, and hoeing, and irrigating pointless?

Absolutely not.

Life lesson: sometimes it hails on our crop. Sometimes it rains on our parade. As difficult as it may be in the moment, when we adopt the mindset of "life is happening *for* us, not *to* us," our eyes are opened and we are able to handle adversity and hardship with more grace.

A personal experience I once had may help to further illustrate this point. As you may know, high school students are required to participate in standardized testing to qualify for potential admission to a university.

There is a test that one typically takes in the United States at the beginning of their senior year called the American College Test (ACT). This test is a big deal because it either guarantees or quickly removes you from consideration to top-tier collegiate universities. The highest one can score on it is 36. For me, this test was going to determine if my application to my college of choice would be heavily considered (they didn't even consider an application if the test score was lower than a 28 unless you were an athlete), or if I would have to face the embarrassment of not being admitted (unlike many of my friends).

The ACT consists of four different timed sections: math, writing, science, and reading.

Growing up I had a knack for writing and reading, but science and math always left my head spinning. It seemed like no matter how hard I tried, or how long I studied, I could never grasp the equations and formulas that so many of my peers were picking up so easily. As one could guess, it's critical to perform well on all the areas of the test or you risk getting a lower score.

When I took the ACT for the first time, I was confident but scared. I didn't study too much, but I thought that I would be just fine because I had gone to eleven years of schooling and figured that whatever was on the test I had previously seen.

Three hours later I walked out with a massive headache. I had no idea what was going on in the math section. There was calculus on the test, and the highest math I had ever gotten to at that point was geometry (again, my peers were far ahead of me in that department). I thought I was going to nail the reading section, but there were one too many prompts I had to get through, which forced me to fill in random bubbles on the test sheet before time ran out.

I got my results back one month later. The verdict: a 19. Again, the highest one can score is a 36. Not good.

"Okay," I thought to myself, "I'll try this again, but this time I'll study."

Two months later I retook the test. I walked out with the same headache, and a couple of weeks later I received my score . . . 18.

"Seriously!?" I wondered. "How could I have gotten a lower score when I studied this time?"

It didn't seem fair, but wasting time complaining about what was fair and what wasn't wouldn't get me into my university of choice. I had to act, so I decided to go for it again.

Final score: 21.

It seemed that every time I took the test, my writing section was scored highest, my science and reading tied, and my math was the lowest . . . by far.

"Welp," I exclaimed, "fourth time's the charm!"

I studied from a test-prep book, I took online practice exams, I went to a tutor, and two months later I walked into the ACT for the last time. I was confident that this would be my saving grace. I would get at least a 28. I had always kept a high grade point average, I tried to be nice to people, I kept my body and mind free from drugs and alcohol, and I didn't cheat or try to take shortcuts in school (except one time in sixth grade but that's a different story). I *deserved* a good grade on this test.

The results came back. Any guesses what my final score was? 30? 32? 34? Close . . . 22.

Four attempts, four tough results. Highest score: 22.

I knew that my chances of being accepted at the university I had dreamed of attending my whole life were slim to none. I had spent years trying to develop my extra-curricular resume. I had received an Eagle Scout award. I had run for senior class president. I had leadership positions in my church. I participated in clubs. I wrote compelling (I think) entrance essays.

But it didn't matter. My test-taking abilities, or lack thereof, would be my downfall. It didn't matter how much I worked, studied, hoped, dreamed, planned, and even prayed—my goal wasn't actualized when I wanted it to be. It had hailed on my crop.

I ended up going to a different university. It wasn't where I wanted to be originally, but it turned out to be the absolute best place I could've been. I excelled in my studies there. I was on different academic boards and counsels. I participated in choir and started a band with my friends. I achieved a GPA after my first year attending there that allowed me the opportunity to reapply to the college I had originally hoped to attend— and I was accepted (probably because I didn't have to retake the ACT. They just looked at my GPA, but hey I'm not complaining!).

No, it didn't happen the way I had hoped.

No, it wasn't according to my timing.

No, it hadn't been easy.

But it helped me learn a valuable lesson: when life knocks us down, it's important to land on our backs because if we can look up, we can get up.

The work that I had put in all those years wasn't wasted—life was simply affording me more time to polish my skills, cultivate my character, and hone my abilities.

The goal I had originally set wasn't actualized when I thought it would be, but who I became in the process of reaching for that goal made me a better person than I would've been had I attained it according to my timing.

Life isn't perfect. Though we may think great thoughts and work extremely hard, life may not go according to our plans. But there's more to life than simply achieving great results. One of my favorite quotes of all time comes from the late Jim Rohn, a business philosopher and motivational speaker. He said, "The major reason for setting a goal is for what it makes of you to accomplish it. What it makes of you will always be the far greater value than what you get" (Rohn, Jim, *Rohn: 5 Simple Steps to Plan Your Dream Life*).

Yes, we work, and we dream, and we hope, and we think good thoughts, and we do the best we can, but sometimes it doesn't work out the way we think it will. Just as Mr. Rohn stated, what matters even more than achieving the objective is who we become in pursuit of it. No, we didn't receive the crop that we wanted, and yes, I bet there will be a few days of discouragement and anger associated with that, but I guarantee that our eight months of preparation wasn't wasted. Think of the skills we've acquired. Think of the character we've developed. Think of the discipline we've built. Think of the fire that is stirring within us to go out and get the best crop we've ever had this next harvest. Think of who we've become in pursuit of what we've wanted.

That's what builds a better life . . . not the results we receive, but who we become in the process of striving for the results we desire.

So, to the potential skeptic who may say that positive thinking won't get us very far, I say, you're right. Positive thinking alone won't get us anywhere, but when mixed with action, purpose, and desire, it will get us farther than negative thinking will. And how we think will determine how we act when adversity strikes, which will determine the outcome of our lives.

Think BIG. Think POSITIVELY. Think CAREFULLY. Then ACT. Don't be naive, and don't *just* hope for things to get better. Poor people hope. Alcoholics hope. Convicts hope. That ought to tell us something. Plan, yes. Dream, yes. Hope, yes. But more important, let us work for what we want. If we get it, great. If we don't get it, learn from it and keep moving. What matters is who we've become in the process.

---— *Chapter 2* ---—

DISEASES OF ATTITUDE

Scientists have approximated that the average human mind thinks 6,200 thoughts a day (Poppenk, n.a.). That's around 390 thoughts an hour (assuming we average eight hours of sleep per night). What are you thinking about? What are you using that precious energy for?

Because all action starts with a thought, we need to be very cognizant of what goes into our minds—and one thing that I've noticed is that it's a lot easier for people to be lazy than to put in the work. It's a lot easier to not care what comes into our minds, whether good or bad, than to stand guard at the door of them with a sword that only lets the good come and stay.

The mind is like a factory. There are lots of pieces moving around, controls being sent, and decisions being made. What we put into this mental factory determines what will come out of the front doors. We choose, however, what ingredients we put into the machines. Are they good, or are they deadly?

Our minds don't care what we put into them. Their job is to mix the ingredients that we put in and produce a result. It's just like planting seeds into the soil. The soil doesn't care what we plant; it only cares about producing a result.

What if we planted tomato seeds, but we wanted raspberries? Answer: we get tomatoes.

What if we *really, really* wanted carrots, and we wished and desired for them to come, but we planted celery seeds? Answer: we'd get celery. It doesn't matter how badly we wanted carrots; we didn't plant carrot seeds!

The same is true with the mind. It doesn't matter how sincerely we hope for things to get better for us or for a positive change in our lives. We reap what we sow. We get what we plant. Good ingredients in, good results out. Garbage in, garbage out, regardless of our intentions.

There are four diseases of attitude that all start with a thought, and I can give you great advice on these because I've had all of them (like I mentioned earlier, we're all on this journey together)! They don't take any real effort to nurture, but the results they produce may be catastrophic in our lives.

1. Pessimism
2. Worry
3. Indecision
4. Neglect

Pessimism

Who likes being around pessimists? Their smile and demeanor just light up a room when they walk in, don't they?

To a pessimist, the glass is always half-empty. They look on the darker side of things, always giving you (or themselves) five reasons something isn't right, won't work, or isn't worth it. They're dream killers. They complain, they whine, and they blame others for the misfortunes of their lives.

They take each disappointment, adversity, or trial with reactions such as, "Why me? Why now? I don't deserve this. This is because my mom did this to me. This wouldn't have happened if my girlfriend didn't tattle on me." And so on. You get the point. As Jeffrey Holland once said, "No misfortune is so bad that whining about it won't make it worse" (Holland, 2007).

Pessimists are better understood with this story I heard once from a minister. When he was on a voluntary service trip in Ireland (which can be very cloudy, foggy, and somewhat depressive for months at a time), there was a day when the sun was shining and the sky was blue. As he and a colleague left their apartment for the day, the minister said, "Wow, look how blue that sky is!"

His colleague responded, "Yeah, I've seen bluer" (S. Tingey, personal communication, 2014).

Lesson learned: don't be like the minister's colleague! We all know people who are like this, and we all know the energy they suck out of a room when they walk in it. Bluntly put, no one likes to be around a pessimist.

Now, that doesn't mean that we go around all day with a fake smile, saying everything is just fine and there's nothing wrong with the world. That's called being naïve. Of course, we need to see reality for what it is, but we can also choose to have hope, faith, and confidence for the present and the future.

Author Alphonse Karr described it this way: "We can complain because rose bushes have thorns, or rejoice because thorns have roses" (Karr, n.a.).

When it comes to problem-solving, the difference between an optimist and a pessimist is how they look at the problem. I'm not suggesting that we always need to be optimistic either. It all depends on our personal philosophy and how we want our lives to turn out.

It's always easier to put someone else down or to say a situation won't work out. Doing those things takes little to no effort.

So, what do we do if we're in a situation where pessimism is present? Choose the higher ground. Choose to uplift. Choose to inspire. Choose to take responsibility for what happens to you and what you become. Choose to face reality, but also choose to speak good into the world and do good in the world, for it will eventually come back to you a hundred-fold.

As the old poem goes, "Two men looked out from prison bars, one saw the mud, the other saw the stars" (Langbridge, n.a.).

Worry

Erma Bombeck, a newspaper humorist and the best-selling author of over a dozen books, described worry this way: "Worry is like a rocking chair. It gives you something to do: but never gets you anywhere" (Bombeck, n.a.).

Need I say more? Worrying is a disease of the mind. It takes a situation that very well may be "figureoutable" and turns it into life or death for the individual.

Someone once said, "Those who don't know how to fight worry, die young." Whether they were referring emotionally or physically, they weren't lying.

I once heard a story of a soldier who was fighting in World War I. His daily duties included going and dragging the bodies of the dead or wounded soldiers off the front lines, and back into the trenches where he would either have to collect personal items to send back to their families or cover their excruciating wounds with bandages and tape while they waited for the medics to arrive. As one can imagine, these responsibilities wore on the soldier greatly and made him ruminate more and more on the possibility of his own death. He worried, and worried, and worried. He worried about getting hit with a bomb. He worried about sending the wrong items back to a dead soldier's family. He worried that his family would forget about him while he was away at war. He worried that his newborn daughter would never get to meet him and that his wife would grow tired of him because she hadn't seen him in over a year. He worried so much that he lost over fifty pounds. He was a walking shadow. He couldn't leave his bunk because he was so weak and exhausted. He would often wake up in the middle of the night with screaming panic attacks that could be heard three tents away.

Then one day he went to see the army doctor. The doctor gave him a thorough physical exam. He checked his heart, his limbs, his eyes, and his ears, and came to this conclusion: the soldier's ailments weren't physical at all. All the panic attacks, all the sleepless nights, and all the weight loss were brought on by mental and emotional anxiety. The doctor then turned to the soldier and gave him this life-saving advice, and I would recommend it to anyone reading this book today:

> I want you to think of your life as an hourglass. You know there are thousands of grains of sand in the top of the hourglass; and they all pass slowly and evenly through the narrow neck in the middle. Nothing you or I could do would make more than one grain of sand pass through this narrow neck without impairing the hourglass. You and I and everyone else are like this hourglass. When we start in the morning, there are hundreds of tasks which we feel that we must accomplish that day, but if we do not take them one at a time and let them pass through the day slowly and evenly, as do the grains of sand passing through the narrow neck of the hourglass, then we are bound to break our own physical or mental structure. (Carnegie, Dale, *How to Stop Worrying and Start Living*, 7)

I used to be a chronic worrier as well. I would worry about school. I would worry about my friend group. I would worry for fear people didn't like me. I would worry about the possibility that I would never marry or be able to provide well for myself and my family. I would worry that my test scores were too low to get me into a good university (we saw what happened there). I would worry, worry, and worry some more . . . and it made me sick. I used to wake up in the middle of the night with sharp, shooting pains in my chest, leaving me reeling on the floor in pain. I came to discover with medical help that these weren't due to physical exhaustion, but mental and emotional stress.

That's the thing with worrying—it gets you nowhere. It takes you round and round in maddening, futile circles. It leads to indecision, not a decision. It leads to inaction, not action.

Those who worry are always asking themselves, "But what if *this* happens?" That question has the potential of ruining an otherwise prosperous, adventurous, and healthy life. If you're always thinking of what could go wrong, you're never going to get very far in life. I promise you that.

"But Drew," someone may say, "how do I *not* worry? I need to worry. Otherwise, nothing will get done in my life. Worrying allows me to get motivated to take on the day and be productive."

To that, I would say, "That's where the importance of this section comes into play. You want to minimize the worry in your life but maximize the concern in your life. Being concerned and being worried are two very different things that lead to two very different outcomes."

For example, if I am so worried that I won't get married, I may do things that are unhealthy, such as overeat, be reckless with my money, stop exercising, binge too much on Netflix, and so on. In other words, being worried about that will lead me to a form of inaction. However, if I am *concerned* about the fact that I may not get married, I will want to develop new skills, maybe think about my future and what a potential spouse would want to see in me, and then get to work to make that future a reality. In other words, being concerned would lead me to action that benefits my future.

Think about when you cross the street. Are you always worried that you won't make it to the other side of the road? Most of the time, no. You're *concerned* that there is oncoming traffic and potential hazards, so you look both ways and proceed with caution.

For those of you who are like me and like to have absolute control over every aspect, person, and event in their lives, I would add this last bit of advice: be concerned about the things you have control over but realize that you cannot control everything. If you can't control something, let it go, have faith, and do what you can do with what you have control over—aka, yourself! (I know, easier said than done).

James Cash Penney, the famed retailer and founder of JC Penney, gave astute advice that I think we should all follow: "I wouldn't worry if I lost every single dollar because I don't see what's to be gained by worrying. I do the best job I can and leave the results in the laps of the Gods" (Carnegie, Dale, *How to Stop Worrying and Start Living*, 77).

Indecision

This is an actual experience that happened in my brain before I wrote this section. *I really should write the indecision section tonight, but I know I need to study for a test tomorrow.* Two hours later. *Okay, maybe I should stop watching Netflix and do something productive with my life.*

I was trying to decide between two good things, so instead of deciding, I chose a much easier (but poorer) alternative . . . Netflix. Can anyone relate?

Indecision can take the form of many things, from laziness to procrastination, but there are usually two emotions that drive it: fear and anxiety.

According to Susan Jeffers, author of *Feel the Fear and Do It Anyway*, when fear or **anxiety** make their appearance during our decision-making (as they always do), the fear is based either on our **belief** that we won't be able to handle the outcome of our decision, or on our doubts about whether we have enough correct information to make the best decision (Jeffers, 2007).

Why is indecision a disease? Because it paralyzes us, halts our growth, and leaves us with a self-esteem crisis because we can never follow through with anything.

I don't know about you, but whenever I struggle with indecision it is because I'm usually in fear that one of my decisions will backfire on me or won't be the *right* decision. Can I get an amen?

Some real-life examples of how I've personally experienced indecision have included:

- Should I buy the store brand of water, or get the Fiji brand for thirty more cents?
- Should I wear my jeans or my khakis to school?
- Should I take my date to Chili's or Olive Garden?
- Should I go to school or take the job offer?
- Should I marry this person or keep dating her?

- Is this job the right job for me, or should I pursue a different route?
- Should we start our family now or wait to be more financially stable?

Obviously, decisions vary in magnitude, but overall, one of the main thoughts that go through the heads of indecisive people is this: "What if one is bad, and the other is good, but I don't know which one to choose? Harder yet, what if both decisions are right, but one decision is *more right* than the other?"

Allow this poem by George W. Bain to answer your inquiry: "The burdens that make us groan and sweat, the troubles that make us fume and fret, are the things that haven't happened yet" (Bain, *Wit, humor, reason, rhetoric, prose, poetry, and story woven into eight popular lectures,* 2012).

Sometimes when it comes to the decision we need to make, the things we fear won't even happen—or aren't even that big of a deal in the long run.

Does it really matter what brand of water we drink? Does it really matter if we wear khakis or jeans to school? Probably not. So why fret about it? Why go through life 'majoring in minor things'? The next time you're in a bind over a decision that is keeping you from acting, apply the 10-10-10-10 rule: *Will this decision affect me in ten minutes, ten days, ten months, or ten years from now?*

If the answer is yes, then study it out, receive the necessary counsel from those wiser than you, and make the best decision you can. If the answer is no, then just decide and move on with your life. You'll be a lot happier, and having mastered the little decisions of life will give you more confidence to tackle the bigger ones.

"Drew," one might ask, "how do I choose wisely when I'm confronted with a big decision? Sometimes I have no idea if what I am doing is right. I feel like I'm walking through life blindfolded, and it makes me not want to act at all."

Those are great thoughts! We've all felt this way, and I still feel this way at times.

The biggest piece of advice that I can offer you is this: Focus on doing the right things with your life (exercise, mindfulness, cultivating relationships, reading/listening to uplifting and inspiring media, prayer, and so on), and then ACT! Gather all the facts you can, seek the insight of those wiser than you (God, family, leaders, friends), and then get up and go do it. If you're honestly trying to do the right things with your life and you have a big decision that you need to make, start moving in one direction and follow your instincts. If it's not right, I'm confident you'll have a stupor of thought, a sick feeling to your stomach, or a divine warning/intervention before you go too far.

In the words of Richard Scott, "When you are [doing your best] and are acting with trust, God will not let you proceed too far without a warning . . . if you have made the wrong decision" (Scott, 2007).

Consider Esther's story when she found out that all the Jewish people in her city were to be killed. Did she sit and stew, or did she go and do? She could've pretended to not know what was going on with the execution order. She could've shut her mouth and allowed the planned injustice to take place. She could've gone to her room, sulked about the impending genocide, and done nothing for fear that she would be killed as well. But she chose the higher road. She got right to work and spoke with her uncle about what she could do to help—and then she ACTED. Did God magically appear with fire and lightning to stop the plan? No. Did He speak to the king for Esther and let her sit back and watch? No. He knew Esther needed this opportunity to decide for herself and act. She took the initiative. She responded. She decided that this challenge wasn't going to be the end. She went to her uncle and said (paraphrasing here), "Mordecai, I love and respect you. I don't know what I can specifically do to help our people, but I want to do the right thing. Now, I need your help and your wisdom. What can I do as queen to save our people?"

Esther's act of faith not only ended up saving her people, but it also taught her and Mordecai a valuable lesson: sometimes injustices happen. Sometimes unfair circumstances that don't make sense or don't seem fair creep up on us. Will we allow them to beat us, or will we rise, decide to act, have faith, and turn a disappointment into an appointment?

John Groberg once said, "Because [life] knows we need the growth, it generally does not point [out the clear direction]. But if [a decision] is wrong, it will let us know—we will feel it for sure. I am positive of that. So rather than saying, 'I will not move until I have this [perfect sense of a destination],' let us turn it around and say, 'I will move unless I feel it is wrong'" (Groberg, 1979).

We have the dignity of choice (as was discussed earlier) for a reason. We have the ability to think, to problem-solve, and to seek knowledge and guidance for a reason. What would be the outcome if every decision was made for us and we were never able to decide for ourselves?

Answer: we'd be living a life of ease and comfort—experiencing no challenges and thus no growth. As the saying goes, "There's not comfort in the growth zone, and there's no growth in the comfort zone."

Thankfully, life allows us opportunities so that we can grow. We can change. We can decide for ourselves which journey we will take. And if we choose to act boldly, decisively, and with confidence, a life of rich fulfillment will be ours for the taking.

Neglect

The last attitude disease that we will address is perhaps one of the most severe. It can rob us of our chances to do well and paint us into a corner of fear, resentment, and disappointment.

American civil rights leader Whitney Young wisely said, "It is better to be prepared for an opportunity and not have one than to have an opportunity and not be prepared" (Young, 1969).

Neglect makes it so that we aren't prepared for life's opportunities. It is the 'I could do it, I should do it, but I won't do it' mentality. That's a recipe for disaster.

What else is something drastic that happens when neglect becomes a factor in our lives?

One word: death.

Here are some questions to illustrate this point:

- What happens to a plant that is neglected and doesn't get enough water and sunlight?
- What happens when a married couple neglects their relationship by being more concerned about their Instagram and Facebook accounts than spending quality time together?
- What happens when you neglect your healthy eating and exercising habits in favor of fast-food, soda, and sitting on the sofa?
- What happens when you neglect to feed your spirit and decide that the latest show on Netflix or the newest video game is more important than prayer, meditation, or reading God's word?
- What happens when your car fuel gauge is on empty but you neglect to get gas before you get on the freeway?

The answer to all of these questions is DEATH.

Without food or sunshine, the plant will die. Without proper growth, communication, quality time, and nourishment, any relationship will eventually die. Without awareness and discipline in healthy consuming and exercising habits the body (and mind) will stop working properly. Without deliberate time spent each day focused on growing our spiritual capacity to receive light, our spirituality will eventually die. Without gas in our cars, they will die.

Now, that doesn't mean if we neglect our health for one day we will immediately see the consequences. Unfortunately, life isn't that black and white. Neglect brings with it a gradual decline, and if we're not constantly vigilant, it may jeopardize our chances of having a successful life.

As Alexander Pope so meticulously explained, "Vice is a monster of so frightful mien, as to be hated needs but to be seen; yet seen too oft, familiar with her face, *we first endure, then pity, then embrace*" (Pope, 1733; emphasis added).

Neglect enters our minds in many ways, and some of the most common thoughts include:

- "That's just too hard."
- "It isn't worth it to push myself that much."
- "I can just do it tomorrow. One day off isn't that big of a deal."
- "I really should do it, but I just don't want to."
- "It would be really good for me to do that thing, but I'm just so tired."

Get the picture? If we have enough days when we say those things repeatedly, our lives will end up in accumulated disaster.

Am I suggesting that we never take a day off? Definitely not. Am I saying that only those who push themselves extra hard find happiness? Heck no! What I am saying is to be aware. Just as we would be extra cautious of a thief who would come in the night to steal our purse, I would suggest that we be just as cautious of the thief that would come anytime to steal our promise and our potential: the promise and potential of a better life, the promise and potential of a more productive future, the promise and potential of a healthier, lovelier, happier, and more beautiful existence.

So, how do we put off the neglect that seems to affect our day-to-day lives more and more?

May I suggest two things: 1) decide *beforehand* what you will do; and 2) understand that what is easy to do is also easy not to do.

First, decide *beforehand* what you will do. Neglect most often shows up in our lives when we don't want to do something. We most often neglect the needful things in life. We put off studying for our test until the last minute, or we decide we aren't going to practice for our recital piece until a week before the program, or we don't crack open God's word or say our prayers until we find ourselves in a major trial.

We need to be prepared for those things, ahead of time.

John Maxwell once said, "It's better to prepare, than to repair" (Maxwell, 2013).

To beat the neglect bug before it beats us, we need to think about what to do before we do it. If our test is in a week, carve out thirty minutes each day to study, instead of a crammed four hours on Saturday. If life is going smoothly for us without any problems, get ready, because a challenge is right around the corner.

Just as autumn follows summer, adversity follows prosperity, and opposition follows success. The time to prepare our spirits is *now* so that when those hard times come, we are ready to face them. If we are in a relationship, we need to nurture it daily because we never know when a problem may arise that will require strength and unity to overcome it.

Second, understand that what is easy to do is also easy not to do.

I used to have the personal philosophy that things were just too difficult for me to do well. I struggled heavily with anxiety and depression at the end of my teenage years, and my attitude was one of gloom and discouragement.

I would look at the motivational biography on my nightstand and say, "I don't want to read today. I'm too sad."

I would look out my window on a beautiful summer day and say, "I really should go running but I don't have the time before work, and I don't want to get all sweaty . . . I just showered."

I would think about my future goals and say, "I really should get out into the world and date, but I'll probably get my heart broken, so I'll just focus on being a bachelor."

You get the point. I was neglectful of the things that would help me feel better, so I chose to do the things that didn't help me feel better. It's easy to exercise. It's easy to go for a walk around the block, or do some push-ups in our living rooms, or take fifteen minutes and do some yoga. Those things are easy. It's also easy to read a good book. It's easy to watch an informative video that teaches us something we haven't learned before. It's easy to take fifteen minutes of uninterrupted time with our spouse or friend to check in on each other, offer each other words of encouragement, and listen to any problems they may be facing. It's easy to pray. It's easy to take ten seconds and thank God that we have a warm home, a car to drive, a heart that beats, a brain that works, or ears that hear. Those things are easy to do!

But, they're also easy not to do, as we've probably noticed in our own lives. It's easy not to do the right things. It's easy not to read. It's easy not to pray. It's easy to ignore the important and focus on the menial. Living in a world of pornography, drugs, alcohol, swearing, division, 24/7 access to sports, drama, Netflix, Hulu, Disney+, and so on, it's easy not to do the things that will bring us long-term joy in lieu of the moment of pleasure that is tempting us. It's easy to say, "I'm just too busy to do those things," or "I just don't have time."

Let me let you in on a little secret . . . we're never too busy for anything.

We always have time for what is a priority to us.

Being busy is a lie we tell ourselves to mask our true problem, which is not prioritizing what really matters to us. We all get the same amount of time every day: 24 hours, 1440 minutes, 86,400 seconds. What separates the person who uses that time to feed their minds, exercise their bodies, and develop their relationships from the person who lounges around all day complaining about their figure, income, self-confidence, or failing relationships?

One word: priorities.

Don't ever say you're too busy or don't have enough time. Say instead, "I've actually decided that I need to prioritize some things over other things, so I can't make the phone call/meeting/party/work. If anything changes, I'll be sure to let you know. Thanks for understanding."

Or, if you've said you'd do something, and you dropped the ball, own it, and don't make excuses! "This was my fault. I am so sorry that I missed the game/meeting/phone call/date . . . Please forgive me, and I promise to make it up to you."

Those who understand that what is easy to do is also easy not to do, understand that everything they do carries consequences. We can either run the day, or the day will run us. We can either decide that we will do the easy things, sacrificing what we want now for what we want in the future, and reap the good life; or we can decide to be "too busy" or "not have enough time" to do the easy things, and eventually we'll come to realize that we've done a whole lot of living, but haven't created a life.

In the words of Jim Rohn, "We all have to suffer the pain of one of two things: the pain of discipline, or the pain of regret. The difference is discipline weighs ounces while regret weighs tons" (Rohn, n.a.).

―――― *Chapter 3* ――――

THE DIFFERENCE BETWEEN SUCCESS AND FAILURE

Thomas Monson once said, "History turns on small hinges, and so do our lives. Decisions determine destiny" (Monson, 2015).

When it comes down to whether we succeed at something or whether we fail, it's usually the small things that make the biggest difference. Rarely, if ever, do we see overnight successes. What we don't realize is that 99 percent of the time, if someone has achieved some major milestone (winning an Olympic medal, publishing a book, overcoming an addiction, getting a promotion at work, and so on), it came from hours and hours of patience, preparation, planning, and persevering.

You may know the story of Michael Phelps, the most decorated Olympian in the history of the world with twenty-eight medals (twenty-three of them being gold). A swimming machine, some have looked at the six-foot, four-inch man and thought, "His physique *looks* like a swimmer. With his long wingspan and double-jointed ankles, knees, and elbows, he belongs in the water."

How do you think he reached the highest pinnacle in athletics? Did he just jump into the water one day, start swimming, and then suddenly he found himself at the Olympics? Not hardly. It took him years of goal-setting, visualizing, swimming, weightlifting, and sacrificing to become great.

For example, when Michael was eight years old, he wrote a goal down. It said, "I would like to make the Olympics."

When he was eleven years old, an Olympic swimming coach spotted Michael and decided to take him under his wing and be his tutor. He noticed Michael's goal-oriented personality and endless drive to become the best he could be and knew that one day he would be an Olympian. According to Michael, there was a five-year stretch throughout his teenage years that he never took one day off. Thanksgiving? Nope. His birthday? Nope. In fact, he would train twice on his birthday. Michael's philosophy was this: "If I am training when everyone else is going to parties, lounging around on the couch, or wasting away on social media, I will achieve what they won't. I know my end goal."

It may sound crazy, but he even trained on Sundays, believing that the extra fifty-two days a year that others weren't training would give him an advantage when it came time to compete.

Now, am I advocating that we forgo every aspect of our lives to pursue our dreams? No. Am I saying that unless we train on Sundays and holidays, we will never reach out dreams? No. What I am saying is that for us to succeed, we'll need to do the things failures won't do. We'll need to set goals. We'll need to visualize our end result. We'll need to work hard and pray hard. We'll need to sacrifice some less important things now for more important things in the future.

One of Michael's greatest assets that he attributed to his success was something that we don't utilize as much as we could in our daily lives: visualization. Visualization is the ability we have to play our goals in our minds like a movie. Every night Michael would lay in bed and visualize himself swimming the entire distance of a race, both from the perspective of someone in the stands and from his own point of view in the pool. He would visualize both best and worst-case scenarios, planning in his head what to do if his suit ripped or goggles broke.

In an interview with a well-known news agency, Phelps credited this part of his training for success in the 200m butterfly at the Beijing Olympics in 2008, where he won gold and set a world record despite not being able to see for the last 75 meters when water filled up his goggles (Owaves, 2018).

That's the power our thinking has in unknown situations. We not only have the ability to think, but we have the power to turn our thoughts into reality.

When I decided to write my first book, *The Meaning of Your Mission: Lessons and Principles to Know You Are Enough,* I was twenty years old. I had just gone through a traumatic experience that left me suffering with severe depression and anxiety. I would often lay on my bedroom floor at night writhing in pain and fear, not knowing when my crippling episode of panic would end. I didn't know that people suffered from these afflictions because they weren't talked about much. Mental illness had a bad stigma around it. You could hear others saying things like, "There's no such thing as depression. Suck it up and stop complaining." Or, "Yeah, I only get depressed when my favorite sports team loses." Or, "Anxiety is just an excuse for not reaching your fullest potential."

It wasn't until I went to therapy and met dozens of people facing the same demons I was that I realized this was a topic that needed to be brought to light. Mental illness, addiction, discouragement, loneliness, heartbreak, same-sex attraction . . . all of these were seen as weaknesses.

So, I started writing my story. I started reading books on depression and addiction and how to cope with difficult challenges. I started listening to podcasts and audiobooks of motivational speakers who would relay to their audiences messages such as, "You have greatness within you!" And, "You can do anything you put your mind to!" And, "Don't let your past determine your future!"

For the first time in months I started to feel like I had control over my destiny, that even though I experienced a traumatic event that left my emotions fractured, and even though I was suffering from an illness that was largely discounted in the culture where I lived, it was legitimate and could be conquered.

I would lie in my bed at night with a pad of paper next to me. While I read a book or listened to a speech, I would write down ideas that came to me or phrases that stood out. I would then close my eyes and imagine myself speaking in front of hundreds of people about my story; about how I was able to overcome my afflictions, find purpose in my suffering, and make meaning of my mission in life. I would visualize the cover of my book sitting on my bookshelf at home, and me picking it up and flipping through the pages, and my little girl running up to me after I had completed a book signing and giving me a kiss on the cheek. I visualized someone coming up to me after I had completed a speaking engagement and saying, "Drew, I never felt good enough until I heard you speak. You've changed my perspective on life. Thank you for all you do."

I played these things on repeat over and over and over again throughout the next four years. During that time, I wrote and rewrote; I planned and prepared; and I failed . . . A LOT. Of the six times I submitted my manuscript to publishers, it was rejected five times. Of the 35,000 words that I wrote in my final manuscript, I had to rewrite 25,000 of them over and over again until I found the right thing to say and the right place to say it. I had to deal with people closest to me saying, "Why are you wasting your time on this, Drew? Just do this, this, and this, and you'll succeed. I did it this way, so you should do it this way."

Let me just stop right there and add something that you may need to be reminded of at this time:

DO NOT LIVE YOUR LIFE BASED ON SOMEONE ELSE'S AGENDA.

DO NOT LIVE YOUR LIFE BASED ON SOMEONE ELSE'S TIME LINE.

SOMEONE'S OPINION OF YOU DOES NOT HAVE TO BECOME YOUR REALITY.

Or, in the words of Ralph Waldo Emerson, "Do not go where the path may lead, go instead where there is no path and leave a trail" (Emerson, n.a.).

I left a trail, and it was based off what was right for me, not someone else.

We must visualize our dreams, plan for the future, work for what we want, and *expect* failure. What? Yes, you read that correctly. Anyone who expects to succeed must come to grips with the fact that they will fail, because in the words of author and coach Scott Miller, "We learn more from our messes than we do our successes" (S. Miller, personal communication, 2020).

It is in the failures that we find the greatest lessons, pieces of wisdom, and motivation to work even harder to achieve our dreams. If I had never been rejected by those five publishers, I would've never made the necessary changes to my manuscript to make it even better. I would never have opened the ten books and added to my knowledge that led to the changes it needed. I would never have felt the pain that comes with not achieving my dreams the first, second, third, fourth, or fifth time—and the drive to succeed that stems from that.

Failing does not make you a failure. You only become a failure when you fail and give up. The same is true of success. Succeeding does not make you a success. It is only when you succeed and continue to show up day in and day out, that overtime, you become a success.

So, to wrap things up, there is a difference between success and failure. Success can be defined as this: a few healthy disciplines repeated every day. You want to succeed as a writer? Write a little every day. You want to succeed as a student? Study every day. You want to get married? Work on making yourself a little more attractive every day. Want to come closer to Jesus? Repent every day.

On the other hand, failure can be defined as this: a few lapses in judgment repeated every day. You want to fail as a spouse? Choose social media over your partner every day. You want to fail as a student? Choose Netflix over your flashcards every day. You want to fail as an athlete? Choose candy and soda over running and water every day. You want to forfeit your chances of living with God again? Choose sin over repentance every day.

It's the little things that make the difference. It was the little things with Michael Phelps, and it was the little things with me.

Work hard.

Plan hard.

Expect to fail—and bounce back after you do.

What matters is who we're becoming, not just what we do.

Chapter 4

TWO PRINCIPLES
FOR A BETTER LIFE

One of the most influential motivational speakers of the twentieth century, Earl Nightingale, gave what I believe to be the greatest definition of success: "Success is the progressive realization of a worthy ideal" (Nightingale, 1957).

There are many different keys to success, and there are no shortages of books out there that claim to contain the "magic recipe" to make all our dreams a reality and all our goals executable. That's not what this chapter is about. My main goal in writing this chapter is to expound on two key principles that may help us with building a quality life and being a little bit better today than we were yesterday.

1. Success is something you attract by the person you become.
2. Life is like the changing seasons.

I grew up in New Canaan, Connecticut. According to various publications, it was in the top twenty richest zip codes in the United States (don't worry, before you judge me as being a preppy rich kid, you can know that my family definitely didn't add to that ranking). There was no shortage of places to look in order to try and become more successful. Within ten minutes from my home lived the CEO of JetBlue Airways, the president of Madison Square Garden, the chief financial officer of Citi Group, one of the most well-known reporters on Fox News, and even a music celebrity.

I thought that if I just did everything those people did, I would one day be successful like them. If I pursued success, as if it were a butterfly,

28

I would eventually catch it and contain it. Unfortunately, that's not how it works. Believe me, have you ever tried to catch a butterfly? It's nearly impossible. You try and be sneaky, tiptoeing after it as if it can't see you . . . then suddenly you lunge at it and it flies away.

Much like success, a butterfly will elude you if you try and chase it. Only when you get busy doing something else will the butterfly come and land right by you, as if it was the one pursuing you.

When we chase after success, it will elude us. Just like we can't get rich by demand (ethically), we can't become successful by demand either.

Success is usually a byproduct of something else we are doing. As we work on ourselves, it will come where we are.

For example, if I make a goal to "become successful," I may waste away my days doing a hundred different things that don't amount to much, instead of focusing on one thing that could make all the difference. On the other hand, if I make a specific goal to "write for thirty minutes a day, five days a week, for three months, and produce at least thirty pages of content," then I will know by the end of that time line if I am successful.

As I mentioned in the last chapter, we can't live our lives on someone else's time line or agenda and expect to attain our fullest potential. We maximize our potential when we discover what our personal mission is and try to live it to the best of our ability.

Key phrase: everything you have now you've attracted by the person you've become. Your possessions, your career, your relationships, your current economic situation, and so on were attracted to you by the person you've become.

Why? Because when we become something better, our lives change for the better. When we take the time to develop our interpersonal skills, master a musical instrument or a specific trade, cultivate an attitude of gratitude and forgiveness, learn how to work with discipline and determination, or practice mindfulness, we are becoming more attractive individuals. And when we become more attractive, life reciprocates with attractive things.

Understanding this principle takes all the pressure off 'outside circumstances' and puts it on the one person that is actually in charge of how their life turns out: YOU and ME. So, do you want to be successful? If the answer is yes, then look at your life and decide how you can attract it. Do you need to read more? Exercise more? Develop a stronger vocabulary? Start taking responsibility for what happens to you? Stop being so hard to get along with? Be kinder? Gentler? It's completely up to you.

Success is 100% subjective.

What success means to me may not be what success means to you. So, here's my advice—don't worry about someone else telling you how you should be successful because chances are their paradigm of success will be different from yours. Look at your life, and if you want to be more successful, start doing the things that you personally believe will make you a more attractive person. Then be amazed at the results you achieve.

Just as the soil doesn't care what a farmer plants, life doesn't care what we plant either. *Life's only job is to produce a result from what* we *plant in it.*

For example, returning to the analogy in chapter 2, what if a farmer *really* wanted carrots but planted tomato seeds? Answer: he'd get tomatoes. What if a farmer *really, really* wanted potatoes but planted beets? Answer: he'd get beets. Just like you can't blame the soil for producing beets when you wanted potatoes, you can't blame life for not giving you the results you want when you're not planting the right ingredients . . . yet so many people blame life for giving them beets instead of potatoes.

Try this for thirty days and see what life gives you. I call it "You Can Have More Than You Got, Because You Can Become More Than You Are."

- Practice gratitude on a daily basis. Find someone to express your appreciation toward, whether it's your spouse, neighbor, parent, sibling, or co-worker.
- Move your body for at least fifteen minutes a day. Remember, when we move our bodies, we change our minds.
- Go for a walk in the sunshine or do some meditation in your bedroom to try and clear your head.
- Do something every day that requires you to think and stretch your mind. Read a book, listen to a podcast, practice a musical instrument, or write a handwritten letter to someone.
- Don't complain or be pessimistic about your life or someone else's. Seriously, just try and go one day (it'll take a while to do a whole month, trust me) without complaining about something. It will help you feel better, and other people will want to be around you more.
- Make your bed in the morning before you leave for the day. Sounds simple, I know, but you'd be surprised how much confidence can come from completing that every day.

I could go on and on, but you get the point. By doing these things we will become more attractive individuals, and our lives will give back more than we could possibly imagine. Try it and live the results.

One final thought on the first key to success: if we can learn to ask and think about the following question, our lives will be healthier, happier, and more fulfilling. *What am I becoming here?*

For example, what do most people ask themselves during a career or a relationship? Usually it's this question: what am I *getting* here?

Don't be focused on getting. Getting is shallow. Getting is temporary. Getting leads to only momentary happiness.

Focus on becoming. Becoming is choosing to nourish the roots of the tree rather than just picking the fruits. Becoming is honorable. Becoming leads to lasting peace and fulfilling experiences in life.

Remember, we don't achieve the good life by focusing on getting something. The good life naturally comes to us as we focus on becoming something better.

There are four major lessons in life to learn, and these are adapted from business philosopher Jim Rohn in his book *The Seasons of Life* (1981). First off, it's so important to study the majors. Isn't it interesting that some people go through life majoring in minor things? And these are the same people that often criticize life for not being 'fair.'

So, as we get into the four major lessons in life to learn, let's first consider these two phrases:

1. Life is like the changing seasons.
2. You cannot change the seasons, but you can change yourself.

Lesson 1: Learn how to handle the winters

Winters come right after falls. How often? Every year since the beginning of history. Some are long, and some are short. Some are warm, and some are bitter. Some are difficult, and some are easy—but they always come right after falls. This is never going to change.

There are all kinds of winters. The winter when you can't figure it out. The winter when your heart is broken into a million pieces. The winter when your prayers seem to go no higher than your head. The winter when your relationships are crumbling and your career is struggling. One writer referred to it as "the winter of discontent" (Steinbeck, 1961).

There are economic winters, social winters, personal winters, spiritual winters, academic winters, and so on.

And just as night follows day, difficulty follows opportunity, and recession follows progression. This is how it's been since the beginning of recorded history, and it isn't going to change.

So, here's the question: How do we learn to handle the winters?

We can't get rid of the season by ripping it off the calendar, but here is what we can do: we can become wiser, more resourceful, and better.

You see, during the winter when I was in my late teens/early twenties, I used to wish it was summer. When it was hard, I wished it was easy. When things would go wrong, I used to blame my circumstances and those around me. How naive. Then, I heard this quote that changed my philosophy on life: *"Don't wish it was easier, wish you were better. Don't wish for less problems, wish for more skills. Don't wish for less challenges, wish for more wisdom."*

I loved it so much, I created my own variation of it that I'd like to share: Don't wish it was easier, *work* to become better. Don't wish for fewer problems, *work* to develop more skills. Don't wish for fewer challenges, *work* to cultivate more wisdom.

We can wish and wish all day long, but if we don't put in the work, then those wishes will stay wishes forever.

So, to sum up this first lesson, remember this: *Yes, the winters won't change, but we can; and that may be the greatest takeaway from this entire book: that for things to change, we need to change. For things to get better for us, we need to get better.*

Lesson 2: Learn how to take advantage of the springs

Spring is hopeful. Spring is like the sun rising after a particularly dark night. Just as the flowers are in bloom, your hopes, dreams, and plans for the future are in full bloom as well.

Spring means opportunity. Opportunity to reflect on your winter and to learn from it. Opportunity to start fresh with new motivation.

There is, however, one caveat to spring: if we don't take advantage of it, we very well could create disastrous circumstances in our lives, because that's the thing with times in our lives when challenges seem to be few and opportunities seem to be many. We slack off; we take our foot off of the gas pedal; we think to ourselves, "Well, if I'm not struggling now, I can just relax."

In fact, this section is a great opportunity for me to make a life-changing declaration to each of you reading this: humans learn life's greatest lessons in one of two ways—inspiration or desperation.

I'll take all your best arguments against that statement but read it once more before you make your case. Note that I didn't say *all* lessons. I said the *greatest* lessons.

Springtime is when we should be learning through inspiration. We should be reading all the books we can, listening to all the podcasts we can, having all the conversations with people wiser than us that we can, moving our bodies so that we can change our minds as much as we can, seeking forgiveness and looking to heal relationships as much as we can, and so on. That's what springtime is for.

Or, we can be lazy, forgetful, stubborn, or careless, and not do any of those things in the spring—and come fall time we'll be experiencing this: desperation. I hate to say it, but it may be too late to repair the damage that's been done in our personal, economic, social, and spiritual lives.

Life is brief. Life is short. And for Heath Ledger, Robin Williams, and Judy Garland, life was extra short. We never know what will happen to us, so we need to use the time we have to prepare and get better.

We need to do the necessary things in the spring, or we will find ourselves destitute in the fall.

Key phrase: plant in the spring or beg in the fall. It's up to us.

Lesson 3: Learn how to nourish and protect your crops all summer

Here are two key phrases to consider under the third major lesson.
First, all good will be attacked.

If you've lived on this planet for very long, you've experienced this. It doesn't matter what *good* you try to do; at some point it will seem almost impossible to do it. Whether it's mental, physical, social, spiritual, or emotional, it will be attacked.

"Well, Drew," someone may say, "you're a downer. I thought this was a section about finding success, not telling me that everything I try and do will be destroyed."

I'd respond to that by asking this: isn't life part negative? Don't we need to be just as aware of the thief who is after our promise, as the thief who is after our purse?

For example, in the human body, we have white blood cells and red blood cells. Red blood cells transfer oxygen and nutrients to all our organs to make sure that the body is well taken care of and working as effectively as possible. White blood cells are in charge of fighting infection. In other words, they're looking for all the attackers that are trying to come in and harm the fragility of life. We need both to function—and neither one is more important than the other.

Ever tended to a garden? The minute we try and make it beautiful and plentiful, the noxious weeds will try to take it . . . and here's something to remember: THEY WILL TAKE IT—UNLESS WE PREVENT IT. The same goes for life. When we start to do something good, evil will pop up out of nowhere and try to stop it. Not to think so is naïve.

Here's the second phrase: all values must be defended.

Social values, political values, friendship values, marriage values, family values, personal values, and business values. Every garden must be tended all summer, for the minute you stop tending it, or become casual in its upkeep, you leave room for all kinds of evil to invade it.

Casualness leads to casualties on the battlefield and in our personal lives.

I was once in a therapy session (therapy is the bomb, and EVERY-ONE should do it at some point in their lives), and the counselor and I were working on ways I could keep negative self-talk from creeping into my life, and instead fill my mind with positivity. In other words, we were working on ways I could more effectively 'tend to my garden all summer.' Contrary to how most therapists would handle this challenge (I know because I've seen many), this person said, "You know what, Drew? You may think that it would only take one thing to keep you from thinking less negatively—meditation, listening to good music, reading something positive first thing in the morning, etc.—but I'm here to tell you that it's not about doing just one thing. The key to overcoming any mental or emotional discouragement is this: constant vigilance."

Constant vigilance.

This doesn't mean that we will never make mistakes or that we won't discover some weeds have grown in our gardens over the course of our summer. That's completely normal and should be expected. What it does mean is that we're disciplined and determined to keep our gardens protected and cultivated until we reap the harvest in the fall.

When it comes to nourishing and protecting our crops during the summer, let us remember that it's not about having a "one and done" mindset, but rather having a long-term perspective, practicing constant vigilance in blocking the evil out, and keeping the good in.

Lesson 4: Learn how to reap in the fall without complaint and without apology

The fourth lesson is all about taking responsibility for what happens to us. One of the highest signs of human maturity is the ability to take responsibility for what happens in our lives.

Part of learning how to reap in the fall without complaint and without apology depends on what you do with your springs. Did you put your nose to the grindstone and give it all you had? Or did you slack off, enjoy the "nice weather" of life, and neglect (one of the attitude diseases) your responsibilities in favor of the easy path?

If you worked hard in the spring and saw your labors rewarded in the fall with a great harvest, celebrate! *Never apologize for working hard and attracting success for yourself.*

There will always be those in your life who, whether because of envy, jealousy, or pitiful self-awareness, will never want to see you succeed and will try to make you feel bad for it when you do. Don't worry about them. Remember, when it comes to criticism, nobody ever kicked a dead dog. The only reason people hate on those who work hard is they're intimidated in some way or another by that success. If we were doing nothing with our lives, the critics would be silent. ENJOY THEM.

On the other hand, let's say you fooled around all spring, and instead of reaping a bounteous harvest in the fall, you saw your labors produce nothing. Let that disappointment and embarrassment propel you to take responsibility. Don't complain. Don't justify. Take responsibility and learn from your mistakes so that you can create something better in the future.

Now, taking responsibility is always easier said than done, and we all would rather have somebody else take responsibility for our actions. But that is not the way to grow.

For example, we've all been in a relationship with or known someone who never takes responsibility for their actions. We've seen them shrug off the consequences of their choices or assign blame to some other external circumstance. These people have low maturity and low self-awareness. They are hard to work with in a professional setting, and they are difficult to tolerate in an interpersonal setting.

If you don't take anything else away from this book, read these words very carefully: *Those who learn how to take responsibility for their actions, regardless of the outcome, will reap the fruits of integrity, satisfaction, fulfillment, and a clear conscious. Those who don't, will walk a lonely way, destitute of all that is worthwhile and joyous in life.*

There's an old African spiritual that says, "It's not my mother nor my father, not my brother nor my sister, but it's me O Lord, standing in the need of prayer" (Rosamond, 2003).

"But, Drew," someone may scream, "you have no idea the disappointments I've experienced! You have no idea the pain and struggle that I've had to unfairly endure. How can you stand here and tell me to take responsibility for things that aren't even my fault?"

Here is what I would say to this person: First off, you are extremely justified in your question, and I'm not trying to downplay your experiences. But here's the thing. We have all felt like that at some point in our lives. We have all felt misjudged, unfairly treated, or at the mercy of the storms of life, and yet there are people who succeed, and people who don't.

How? Because those who succeeded discovered and utilized these two key principles:

First, success is not something you chase. Success is something you attract by the person you become (which we discussed earlier in this chapter).

Second, it's not what happens to you in your life that determines the quality of your future. It's what you do with what happens to you.

What happens to one of us, happens to all of us. The sun went down on everybody last night. I've learned personally that two of the same things can happen to two different people, and one gets bitter and the other prospers. Why is that? It's because they both responded differently to the adversity. In other words, one took responsibility and turned a disappointment into an appointment, and the other shrugged off responsibility and focused on how unfair life was to them. Which person will we be?

---— *Chapter 5* —---

IT'S ALL ABOUT RELATIONSHIPS

It's been said in years past that, in a business setting, "The greatest asset a company possesses is its people." That has now been replaced with, "The greatest asset a company possesses is the *relationships* between those people" (Davis, 2017). If Tammy and Ben can't get along with each other, then it doesn't matter how great they are individually—the culture will sour, and the initiatives will suffer.

The same is true in our personal lives. The relationships that we share with those around us mean everything, and without them we are nothing. For example, when your relationship with someone suffers, how difficult does it make everything else in your life? When a relationship is strained, be it between spouses, parent and child, mother-in-law and daughter-in-law, brother and sister, boss and employee, and so on, everything else in life is strained. Things are more stressful, the bills seem stacked higher, things you found fulfilling become hollow, rebellious decisions become more frequent, test scores get lower, and you wish with all your heart that the issue would just resolve itself.

This chapter aims to give three foundational principles that, if applied, will help us become better and more attractive individuals—thus giving us the tools to influence our relationships for the better—because life is all about relationships.

The Relationship with Yourself Is Key

Before I discuss anything else concerning relationships, it's necessary that everyone reading this section understands that if we don't create a good relationship with ourselves first, then all our other relationships will be shallow and hollow. Everyone knows someone who prides themselves on being so service-oriented that they often collapse at the end of the day proclaiming, "Oh, if I just had a little bit of time for myself, how much happier I would be!"

Well, that's the point of this section—to help us understand that for our other relationships to be healthy, for our service-oriented mindset to grow and flourish, we need to take care of numero uno (ourselves).

Just think about how a relationship between two spouses could change for the better if each of them took time every day to feed their minds, their bodies, and their spirits. Think about the good that could come if both individuals increased their spiritual, emotional, physical, and intellectual capability by two, three, or five times. Think about what that could do for their friendship, their marriage, and their futures together.

Now, some may say it's selfish to focus on yourself. They may argue that those who spend time on themselves are petty, insecure, over-dramatic, and too sensitive. They may be right . . . to a certain extent. Spending five hours on social media or video games a day all in the name of "self-recharge time" is not healthy. It's also not healthy to neglect your spouse, children, work, or civic/ecclesiastical responsibilities to spend three hours doing "your own thing" when you know you are needed elsewhere. That's a sign of immaturity. That shows a lack of self-awareness.

For example, my wife has a friend who became a first-time mother at the end of 2019. Her child was born with complications that resulted in numerous surgeries and thus required a lot of time, energy, and money to be taken care of. Her husband used their baby as an excuse to not be around when he was needed most. He would say, "I need to work all day so that we can pay for these hospital bills, so I can't take feed/change/play with the baby." He would frequently come home from work around 5 pm, proceed to put on his workout clothes, would go to the gym for an hour, and then get home and say to his wife, "Okay, now I need to take some time for myself. I've had a long day and I need to recharge." He wouldn't help with their newborn child until 8 pm, creating a massive crater in their marital relationship that has resulted in an unending series of conflicts.

We see here that we can unhealthily take care of ourselves too much, especially when it comes at the expense of our loved ones.

Here are some unhealthy activities that will hinder our ability to create a good relationship with ourselves:

- Spending hours and hours in front of a computer or TV screen playing virtual games.
- Viewing pornography.
- Checking Instagram and Facebook every quiet moment we get during the day.
- Neglecting family, civic, or professional responsibilities and doing "our own thing" for hours a day.
- Hanging out with friends every night instead of taking time to just be alone with ourselves.
- Having music constantly playing in the background whenever we're driving, walking, or relaxing.

It's my opinion that many people in the twenty-first century are uncomfortable with silence. We are uncomfortable with stillness. Because of technology our brains have been programmed to stimulate us every time we hear a ding, beep, or click. And when those notifications aren't going off we feel uneasy and unsettled, so we force ourselves to do something that will actually make us unhappy in the long run (checking social media, watching Netflix, or just trying to be busy doing something unnecessary) instead of just choosing to be bored for a few minutes.

Allow yourself to be bored.

The next time you go for a drive with your spouse or partner, or the next time you leave the room for five minutes or go to bed, unplug from your phone or tablet. Let yourself experience the peace and quiet that comes from being distant from the world for just a few minutes. It'll be very uncomfortable at first and may even cause a mini panic attack, but slowly you'll start to realize that you're happier and less stressed without the constant pressure that comes with being buzzed and binged 24/7.

Now, in terms of building a healthy relationship with ourselves, taking short bursts of undivided time every day to recharge, refocus, and rejuvenate our own emotional, physical, spiritual, and mental gas tank is a sign of maturity. It is a sign of high self-awareness. Why? Because we're showing ourselves, and those around us, that we care enough about ourselves to become wiser, stronger, and better.

Here's another example. I have a close friend who serves as an executive vice-president at a management consulting firm. His job requires him to be "on" from 5 am to 5 pm. He needs to be on multiple phone calls with clients, participate in podcasts and webinars, and follow through on his daily commitments as a member of the executive team. It would be very easy for him to neglect his family, civic, and ecclesiastical responsibilities all in the name of "recharging" when he gets home, but he makes sure to be very deliberate around what he calls "the most important things." He'll make sure to text his high-school kids in the morning before they go to school, he'll call his wife at lunchtime to see how her day is going, and when he gets home everyone knows it's "personal time" for an hour. From 5 to 6 pm he'll go for a run, read a book, watch TV, or do something that allows him to refocus. This makes it easy for him to come back to his family refreshed and rejuvenated to help with dinner, play with his kids, and spend quality time with his wife. By taking time each day to develop a relationship with himself, he is a better dad, spouse, and employee.

Here are some healthy activities that will increase our ability to create a good relationship with ourselves:

- Reading a book.
- Writing in a journal.
- Taking time to be still and listen to whatever is going on around us (birds chirping, cars driving by, the washing machine going, and so on).
- Going for a walk, run, or bike ride outside in the sunshine (or indoors if it's cold).
- Praying or meditating.
- Watching an episode or two of our favorite show to ease our stress and laugh about something.

Remember, moderation in all things. We don't want to spend five hours a day reading a book or working out in the gym because we think it'll make us more attractive people and will thus benefit our relationships with others. We also don't want to spend five hours a day on Netflix or napping, making the excuse that we need a break and can't handle anything else without recharging.

If you are single, decide for yourself what the best way is for you to develop a better relationship with yourself. If you have a family, get together with them and discuss ways that everyone can support each other in taking time for their individual development and health every day.

You'll be blown away by the results you start to see as you, and those you love, take time every day to healthily build relationships with yourselves.

Carry Your Own Weather (Be Proactive)

Popularized by Stephen R. Covey in his bestselling book, *The 7 Habits of Highly Effective People* (Covey, 2020), this concept of carrying our own weather became a hallmark for those who want to change themselves and their relationships for the better.

It's quite a simple principle: those who carry their own weather don't allow outside circumstances to interfere with their internal peace, or in other words, they're proactive instead of reactive.

Carrying our own weather means that we don't get offended easily, that we forgive without holding a grudge, that instead of metaphorically beating someone over the head with their shortcomings, we look within ourselves and think about times when we've been hard to get along with, difficult, short, or annoying, and we realize that what the other person did isn't all that bad because we've made similar mistakes in our lives.

Now, this doesn't mean that we walk around with rose-colored glasses on, seeing everything as wonderful and perfect even in times of grief and despair. But it does mean that we don't allow the negativity around us to penetrate our souls to the point that we become absorbed by it.

My dad is a great example to me of someone who carries their own weather. Ever since I was a little boy, he has shown me that regardless of what is going on "out there," you can be cool, calm, and collected—or at least appear like you are. You see, growing up in one of the richest zip codes in all the United States, my parents sometimes struggled to make ends meet. The employer that moved my dad from Utah to Connecticut had to abruptly let him go after 9/11, leaving him with no income and five kids at home (and three kids out of state) to take care of.

Did my dad come home with his tail between his legs, pouting and complaining about how insensitive his employer was, or mope around the house like life owed him more than he was getting? No. Now, in the privacy of his own car or bedroom he may have been sad or disappointed, but he never let us see that.

What did he do? He went out and got a job at a call center. That's right. An accomplished, six-figure earning, university graduate, living in one of the most expensive zip codes in the United States with five mouths to feed went out and got a job at a call center in order to try and make ends meet while he looked for greater opportunities.

Instead of being reactive about his circumstances, he decided to take the higher ground and be proactive. Was it easy? No. Did we struggle financially for a few months? Yep. Did we eventually pull through due to my dad's unending resolve and optimism? Yes.

Because my dad knew in his soul that for things to change for him, he had to change, he went out and got busy doing the things that would make a positive impact on his future. He knew that life didn't owe him anything. He lived the principle: carry your own weather.

Now, on the other hand, there are those that become affected by everything. If they wake up and look outside and it's cloudy, the day is ruined. If they see that someone "read" their text message but didn't respond, they think they're hated and annoying. If one of them got into a fight with their spouse before they went to family dinner, EVERYBODY is gonna hear about it and know that they are MAD.

Know anybody like that?

One person comes to my mind for this part: I'll call them Taylor. I've known Taylor for a couple of years now, and almost every single time I've seen them they've had something or someone to gripe and complain about. It doesn't matter if it's their job that they think they don't get paid enough in, or if it's a certain relationship that they feel mistreated in, or that one of their pets is just too crazy. Taylor will let you know about it and will bring the overall "happiness meter" down in the room at the same time. Taylor demonstrates a very reactive personality where for them to be nice, you need to be nice; for them to be respectful, you need to be respectful. They need a wonderful relationship, a high-paying job, and no external problems, or else it's like the world is ending.

Why? Because they haven't figured out that they are 100 percent in charge of what happens to them and how they respond to those circumstances. They haven't discovered for themselves that those who are most successful and happy with their lives aren't always searching for external validation, but seeking to develop themselves, their skills, and their attractiveness, creating internal validation and fulfillment.

Now, before I get people putting the book down because I'm being too harsh, I'm not saying that it's a sin to complain every once in a while, or to vent about your problems to trusted family and friends. That is actually healthy and is part of being human. But when those problems absorb you to the point that you need to bring everybody else down around you who seem happy and content—that's when it's a major issue.

So, how do we develop this skill of carrying our own weather? Be like my dad and don't be like Taylor. More sincerely, do the following:

- Be more mindful of your thoughts and your words. Try and catch yourself when you find yourself blaming everything "out there" instead of thinking about the one thing you can control—yourself.

- *Ask someone close to you, "What is it like to be in a relationship with me? Do I help you become stronger, better, wiser, happier? Or do I tear you down?" Then listen to their answer and apply it.*

- Understand the fact that proactive people are those who focus on being solution providers, not problem identifiers.

Don't Hate—Appreciate

For anyone who has ever read arguably the most influential book ever written on creating better relationships, *How to Win Friends and Influence People* (1936) by Dale Carnegie, you know that appreciation is one of the noblest of virtues, while tearing others down is one of the lowliest of human capabilities.

Appreciation is the crowning jewel of any task completed.

Everybody loves to be appreciated. It doesn't matter how menial the chore or how grand the gesture—those who appreciate others for what they do to and for them will never lack for superb relationships.

One of the first people in American business to earn a salary in excess of one million dollars a year (when most people were taking home fifty dollars a week) was Charles Schwab. He had been hand-picked by Andrew Carnegie (one of America's most well-known steel magnates) to be the first president of the newly formed United States Steel Company in 1921.

Why did Mr. Carnegie pay Charles so much? Was it because Charles had a PhD? Was it because Charles was his nephew? Was it because Charles had twenty years of experience in steel?

None of those. He picked Charles because he knew how to inspire and motivate his employees. He knew how to deal with people.

He said, "I consider my ability to arouse enthusiasm among my people the greatest asset I possess, and the way to develop the best that is in a person is by appreciation and encouragement. There is nothing else that so kills the ambitions of a person as criticism from superiors. I never criticize anyone. I believe in giving a person incentive to work. So, I am anxious to praise but loath to find fault. If I like anything, *I am hearty in my appreciation and lavish in my praise*" (emphasis added).

Contrary to what Charles did, what do most people do? They find fault. They point out the flaws. They think that if they compliment or praise too much, it'll start to "go to the head" of the other person and produce negative consequences.

Let me just say this: we can never compliment or find something praise-worthy in someone too much. In a world that finds humor and fulfillment in seeing other people's "fail videos," breakup stories, and relationship dramas, we all need someone who will give us sincere praise and appreciation. Notice that I said "sincere." Praise that isn't sincere or lacks authenticity will backfire on you very quickly.

Growing up, I had a friend whose father would find fault with every-thing my friend did. His dad would give each of the children a chore-chart for the week. Each day consisted of different vacuuming, sweeping, toilet-cleaning, or bed-making responsibilities that needed to be completed before they went out to play with friends. My friend was naturally obedient, so he made sure to do his very best on the chores each day. At the end of the task he would go down to his dad's office and say enthusi-astically, "Dad! I just finished the bathroom upstairs. Can you come look at it so I can go outside and play?"

His dad would make his way upstairs, step into the bathroom, and the first words out of his mouth would be, "The mirror still has spots on it. You didn't get in the corners near the bathtub. You missed over here by the sink."

All critique, no praise.

And it crushed my friend. All he wanted was for his dad to be proud of him for the work he tried very hard to do. He wasn't afraid of his dad telling him of some things that needed improvement, but to not even have mentioned the things he did well took a toll on him. It bled into a perfec-tionist complex that my friend was challenged by for years. He never felt like anything he did was good enough because of how his dad treated the work he did growing up.

Now, does that mean we never introduce others to their own blind spots or point out things that are done wrong? Of course not. Espe-cially in a professional setting, constructive feedback can be revolu-tionary to benefit someone's career. But, in a personal relationship? How often do you like to be told that you're doing something wrong, or that what you did wasn't good enough? For me, it's an immediate turn-off. The key is to create an environment and culture of trust and love within your relationship, so that the *other* person asks you for feedback. Then you can give them sincere, honest, and (hopefully) constructive ideas that will be taken in the right way.

As the old poem by Dale Carnegie goes, "Once I did bad and that I heard ever/ twice I did good, and that I heard never."

It seems to me that most of us have this false mindset that by taking time to lift others up with appreciation and praise, we are somehow diminished. That's completely false.

Schwab also said, "In my wide association in life, meeting with many and great [individuals] in various parts of the world, I have yet to find the [individual], however great or exalted [their] station, who did not do better work and put forth greater effort under a spirit of approval than [they] would ever do under a spirit of criticism."

So, what is the moral of this section?

- We can't force anyone to give us *sincere* appreciation, but what we can do is be an example of, first and foremost, showing it toward others.
- Focus on creating an environment of trust, respect, and admiration in your relationship, and then watch your spouse, work colleague, partner, significant other, and so on come to YOU seeking your feedback and advice.
- For every critique you'd like to give someone, first find three praiseworthy items to give them. Then see if that critique is even that big of a deal.
- Don't be sarcastic, petty, or insincere in your praise, appreciation, or admiration. People will see right through you.
- Don't show appreciation to someone so that they'll show appreciation to you.

— Chapter 6 —

ENLIGHTENED SELF-INTEREST

All of us have self-interest. Simply put, it is our innate desire to get things, and to do it even at the expense of those around us: wealth, acclaim, food, water, shelter, love, power, glory, admiration.

The point of this chapter is not to discourage or dissuade us from having self-interest but to encourage us to turn that into *enlightened* self-interest so that everybody wins and nobody loses.

Our first interest is to survive. Our greatest biological craving is to survive, even if it's just from one minute to the next.

Our second interest is to succeed. We have an innate desire to be successful. We crave the satisfaction that comes from doing the best we can at something and seeing the harvest that follows it.

Can we both survive and succeed? Can we be as interested in succeeding as we are in surviving—and help others do the same?

YES! We can survive and succeed both as individuals and a community, but what is needed to do so is not just self-interest, but enlightened self-interest.

Key phrase: life wasn't designed to give us what we need—life was designed to give us what we deserve.

We don't reap a harvest in the fall because we need it. We reap a harvest because we deserve it. Just as there are moral laws, and physical laws, this too is a law.

If we were to go to the fields in the fall, not having worked and plowed during the spring and summer and expecting a full harvest, what do you think the ground would say to us?

Who is this fool who brings me their need but brings me no seed?

Deserving a plentiful harvest is not done by bringing our need to the field. It's done by bringing our seed to the field. The same goes for our everyday lives. It's not enough to bring our need to the marketplace, our marriage, our work, or our community that starts the deserving process; it's bringing our seed, our effort, our willingness, our determination, and our sacrifice that starts the deserving process.

Reaping is reserved for the planters, and the reason they reap is they deserve it—because they put the time and effort into sowing the seeds of ambition, determination, and deliberate action.

The Bible discusses the idea that if we keep knocking, we'll discover open doors (Matthew 7:7-8); doors of opportunity, doors of fulfillment, doors of excitement, doors of success, doors of relationships and enterprises. We don't discover these open doors because we need them; we discover them because we deserve them.

If we search, we will find (see Matthew 7:7–8). Finding is reserved for the searchers. At first, they may have needed it, just as we all have needs, but ultimately, they found what they were looking for because they searched, they inquired, they pursued, and so on. We've got to go to church, we've got to go to class, we've got to go to the library, we've got to go to the seminar, to the gym, to the lab. We must first put in the effort to search out good ideas, good philosophies, good health, good spirituality, and good advice, and once we've searched (and researched), the answer is sure; we will find.

Key phrase: rarely does a good idea interrupt us. Seldom, if ever, does the lazy person receive an answer to a question or inquiry. (Notice how I said lazy, *not* meditative *or* contemplative). *Answers require action, and action requires preparation.*

The reason you'll be blessed with good ideas as you read this book is that you've come searching for them. You didn't read this far in the book because you felt obligated (thank you, Mom), or because you thought it was a book on baking decadent cakes. You are on this page because you came searching for something, and because you've put in the effort, I am confident what you're searching for will be revealed.

Next, it says that those who ask, achieve (see Matthew 7:7–8). This is one of the greatest lessons I've ever learned in my life.

We will never achieve anything worthwhile by our own individual efforts. Every great thing that has ever been attained or acquired in this life came because of a communal effort. It came because someone asked somebody else for help, for guidance, for love, for care, for advice.

When I was twenty-three years old, I was working at the advisement center where I went to college. I was earning ten dollars an hour to help develop curriculum, design apps, and mentor students in various student development courses. I loved what I was doing, but it wasn't helping me enough economically to support my family. I knew I needed to find something else, but I didn't know how. I hadn't graduated college, I had never worked at a major company before, and I didn't have a lot of experience in business, marketing, or finance.

But, guess what I was?

I was hungry!

I was eager!

I was willing to put myself out there and ask someone for help.

Was I afraid? No. Because what did I have to lose? I would've stayed in the same place, earning the same income, doing the same things. I had nothing to lose. So, one day I went onto LinkedIn, updated my profile with my experiences, internships, and achievements, and started sending personalized messages to anyone who had a vice-president or above title in my desired field of work. I sent dozens and dozens of messages, listing why I admired the work these men and women had done in their careers, why I admired their company, and how I could add value through my experience to their business.

Within three days I had half a dozen responses from chief executive officers, executive vice-presidents, and owners of companies, expressing their willingness to help me out, and their admiration that I had taken the initiative to reach out.

Over the next week I had three interviews and landed myself an internship paying thirteen dollars an hour. I worked my tail off for the next two-and-a-half months, working on various projects, getting people lunch for meetings, picking up dry-cleaning, and learning as much as I could, and earned an offer to become a full-time salaried employee.

Within three months, I went from earning ten dollars an hour to working full-time at a prestigious leadership development firm in Salt Lake City, Utah. Did I have a college degree? No. Did I have internship experience at a company with 10,000 employees and $1 billion in revenue? No. Did I have glowing recommendations from millionaires? No.

Did I sit around and sulk and wonder why I couldn't be paid more for the work I was doing at the advisement center? No.

Here's what I did do. I acted. I asked for help. I decided to be in control of my destiny. I knew that nobody was going to reward me for something I didn't earn.

Did I do something that makes me better than my work colleagues, or college friends, or somehow elevates me to "genius level"? Absolutely not. Anyone could do what I did. It doesn't take anything more than a willingness to put oneself out there and develop a work ethic that will outdo one's current level of experience or knowledge.

I learned four major lessons from this experience:

1. People are more willing to help you out than you think.
2. What stops most people from asking is the fear of being rejected or appearing weak.
3. Asking is the beginning of obtaining and lays the groundwork for deserving.
4. Unless you're a newborn child or a spoiled teenager, you'll never obtain anything of value in this life unless you ask for an opportunity to work for it.

To all the parents out there, here is a good lesson of how this can be used in a family setting. Let's say a child approaches you and says, "I need ten dollars."

Most parents might just give the child ten dollars or turn them away with a remark about how they can't afford to give them ten dollars.

But you're not most parents. You're wise, smart, and extremely intelligent because you're reading this book at this moment—so I'll give you the secret.

Here's the key way for an adult to reply to the child's request: "Hold up. That language doesn't work here. There's plenty of money, and the vaults are full, but you must learn that life doesn't give us what we need—it gives us what we deserve."

The young child learns then and there a very powerful lesson that will influence the remainder of their lives: how to ask correctly so that they open the vaults to receiving.

Here's the question: "How can I *earn* ten dollars?"

That's the key. As the child learns how to earn, they will come to find that they deserve what they receive.

Lastly, the Bible says those who give, receive (see Luke 6:38). Now, to the uneducated individual that philosophy may seem backwards. How could those who give, receive? It's an oxymoron. As mentioned at the beginning of this chapter, the basis of human self-interest is to receive. Period. It's not to give. That's why we are discussing the idea of *enlightened* self-interest, because only in giving can we fully open the doors to receiving.

Remember: receiving is reserved for those who give; and those who give the most receive the most in return.

One may say to that statement, "Well, I can only take care of myself!"

That's okay. Self-preservation is okay. Self-defense is okay. Self-care is okay. Self-interest is okay. But they won't reap the long-term benefits that taking care of others along the way brings. They won't provide the good life that we've been discussing throughout this book. The good life only comes when we focus more on giving than receiving, or in other words, the secret to living is giving.

Someone once asked a great question: "How can I become great?" (Matthew 20:20–28).

The answer: learn how to serve the many.

More simply put: service to many leads to greatness.

How can we become noble? How can we become powerful and create a valuable influence for the world? Find ways to serve as many people as we can.

As the remarkable Zig Ziglar once said, "The way to get whatever you want is to help enough other people get what they want" (Ziglar, 1978).

Think of some of the most influential people in the history of the world:

- Nelson Mandela
- Mother Teresa
- Harriet Tubman
- Winston Churchill
- Eleanor Roosevelt
- Martin Luther King Jr.

What do all these people have in common? They each found ways to serve a lot people. They each found ways to give others purpose and inspiration in one way or another, and in return they grew their own influence.

Now, some may read this and be thinking to themselves, "I really want to be great, and I really want to serve a lot of people, but I don't know where to get started. It seems like I only have the resources to take care of myself right now."

Here's another good phrase from antiquity to help increase your understanding: *Be faithful when the amounts are small* (see Matthew 25:23).

You can't expect to be given dominion and influence over others when you first haven't even mastered yourself, right? The key is to start on you. Be faithful to your own personal development. Take responsibility for your own growth. Look at your life and decide how you can become a more attractive person. Then as you become better, wiser, and more valuable—or in other words, as you show to yourself and others that you *deserve* to serve a lot people, your ability to reach and inspire those around you will grow.

In conclusion of this chapter, let's remember these key phrases:

- Life wasn't designed to give us what we need; life was designed to give us what we deserve.
- Those who knock will discover open doors.
- Those who search (and research), will find.
- Those who ask will obtain.
- Those who give will receive.

—————— *Chapter 7* ——————

IT'S POSSIBLE

As you go through this chapter, I want you to start thinking about a major goal that you'd like to achieve. Maybe you've been working on it for some time. Maybe you've given up on that dream due to unforeseen challenges and setbacks. Maybe you've wanted to start working on it but don't know quite where to begin.

The first thing to remember is this: there are winners in life, there are losers in life, and there are those who have not yet discovered how to win. And all they need is some coaching, a little encouragement, support, and guidance to access the unlimited power that they have locked within themselves.

So, as you think about something that you want in life—something that is real for you, something that is meaningful for you, something that will give your life special purpose and direction—all I want for you to say, "It's possible."

I don't even want you to say, "I can do that."

You see, when I was nineteen, I didn't even know I could write, and I couldn't even fathom that I'd be a published author of two bestselling books at the age of twenty-five. It would've been too much of a mental leap for me to just assume it was going to happen, or that I could reach this level.

No, I don't want you to assume that it's just going to happen. I don't want you to psyche yourself out. I don't want you to read this book and proclaim to the world that in a year's time you're going to be a published author, or the CEO of your company, or an Olympian athlete, or whatever your dream is—not because you *can't* achieve your dream but because in the process of pursuing what you want in life there are going to be setbacks and disappointments, and most people will give up if their time line isn't met exactly when they say it will be.

For example, I grew up in family that are members of The Church of Jesus Christ of Latter-Day Saints, a religion where service is highly valued and expected—so much so that when a male turns eighteen years old, he is expected to serve a two-year mission. This entails leaving his family, taking all he can fit in a suitcase, and going to an assigned location where he will serve and teach those interested in learning about Jesus Christ. Though it may not seem like it, it's a BIG deal—and with it comes almost incalculable expectation.

This was a dream of mine ever since I was a young boy. I watched three of my older brothers serve honorable missions, and I had countless friends who served missions as well. When I was nineteen, I received my assignment to serve in an area in eastern Europe, and leading up to my assigned departure date I had hundreds of people who knew about it—through my own efforts and those closest to me spreading the word. The night before I left, I even posted on social media that I would be leaving for two years and that I was looking forward to seeing everyone when I got back.

I had a goal, and my goal was to serve two years, without setbacks, and come home an entirely changed person.

Well, it didn't work out like that. Though I did serve, it was only for two months. I came home early due to mental illness that ended up crippling me for the following four years.

I didn't accomplish my goal. I had set such a rigid time line, and EVERYONE knew about it. When it didn't happen, I was seen as a failure. I was disappointed in myself, and those who loved and supported me before I went were disappointed as well.

Though painful, this experience taught me a valuable lesson: yes, goals are important. Dreams are crucial. In fact, there's a famous Bible verse that says, "Without vision people perish" (Proverbs 29:18).

But we need to be careful how we set them up in our minds. We need to be aware of what we are setting ourselves up for if we don't hit them, or if something beyond our control hinders us from reaching the goal in the way or time we had anticipated. We need to be thoughtful of how we broadcast our goals to others because if we decide to tell hundreds of people about them, we will need to live with the results of everyone knowing whether we've succeeded or failed. For me, everyone knew that I had high expectations to complete my goal, so when I didn't complete it, everyone knew I didn't.

This doesn't mean that I am not grateful I set the goal in the first place, or that I had high expectations. As we learned earlier, the main reason of setting a goal is what it will make of us in the process of reaching for it. The point is that I should've been more mindful about how I set and broadcast the goal and what I expected from it.

That being said, there's something we can do every day that will help us, slowly but surely, start to become a little bit better, start to reach a little bit higher for our dreams, and start to enable us to maintain a level of integrity with ourselves.

This is something for us to focus on when we've got an idea/goal/dream we want to accomplish. We might not have the money, we might not have the education, we might not have the support or the resources we need. What is that something that can keep us going, that will enable us to act on our dream?

We must say this to ourselves every morning: "It's possible!"

Having this mindset, even when we experience setbacks and unforeseen challenges, will be enough to keep us in the game—to keep us reaching for our goal. We all have certain belief systems in life—things we believe are possible for us, impossible for us, or anywhere in between. Most of the time, when we start to go for a certain goal, we are met with a lot of self-doubt and negative self-talk.

The way we act is a manifestation of what we truly believe is possible for us. Everything that we've done up to this point in our lives is a duplication or a reproduction of what we think is possible for us; what we believe we deserve in life.

Do you think you're blessed and highly favored, deserving of the greatest thing's life has to offer? Or do you subconsciously feel like you aren't good enough and that everything you've earned up to this point in your life is because of "luck" or coincidence?

Your answer to these questions can tell you a lot about what your current belief system is at this present moment. You see, most people operate out of their personal history, their memory, their past. They act based on things that they have already done, experienced, said, felt, or seen another person experience. They look at when they were five years younger and five years less mature and think that because of where they were then and the mistakes they made, they can't reach their goal now. Because they tried to conquer that addiction to drugs, alcohol, or pornography back then and failed, they can't possibly conquer it now. Because they made the leap to have a relationship with a wonderful partner but it didn't work out the first time, they think they are unworthy of ever finding love again. Because they failed the entrance exam to their university of choice the first time, it's not even worth it to try a second time. Have you experienced anything like this before?

Key phrase: use the past as a school to teach you, not a hammer to beat yourself up with. Learn from your past, but don't let it destroy your present or your future.

What I'm suggesting is that you operate out of a larger vision for yourself. Look at where you want to go and stay focused on that destination.

Act out of your imagination, not your memory.

Why? Because when you start declaring to yourself that it's possible for you to have what you want, you are going to feel a lot of adversity, temptation, and distraction. You are going to get caught up with what I just explained, believing that you can't have what you want because you're not worthy of it, or you've made too many mistakes, or you didn't get it the first time so how could you get it this time. Your memory may cause you to doubt yourself.

When I was nineteen years old, I started writing my first book. It all began when I was asked to share my experience dealing with mental illness to a group of about fifty individuals. I wrote down some notes on what I wanted to share, and afterward I decided to use those notes to write a manuscript. I had never thought I'd write a book, and to be honest I never really had any desire to. But I did want to add value to other people's lives, and I thought that this would be a good way to do that.

I wrote and rewrote, edited and reedited for about two years, and then I submitted it to a publisher.

I was rejected.

They didn't give me any feedback on what needed improving, so I went back to the drawing board and reviewed the manuscript. I noticed little things that I thought could be changed or expounded upon, so I rewrote them and resubmitted it about six months later.

I was rejected again.

At this point I was very distraught. I had spent hundreds of hours pouring out my soul into this manuscript, having to relive some very painful experiences in my life as I struggled to put my thoughts of dealing with the abyss of mental illness into words.

I had a lot of self-talk telling me that I should just stop trying. I had been rejected twice. Why try again? I wasn't even a writer and didn't really know what I was doing, so if I stopped no one would've ever known . . . except me. And that is what propelled me to keep trying.

This time I asked for professional help from a university professor. He helped me edit and proofread the manuscript. Six months later I submitted it again.

I was rejected yet again.

This time they did have some feedback for me: "It's too much of a niche topic. We don't think it will sell very many copies."

That fired me up! I was going to show them that it would sell and that it would become a bestseller! (By the way, it did become a bestseller and ended up selling more than 1,000 copies in the first month.)

I went back again, and again, until finally on the sixth attempt to publish, I saw these words in an email: "Drew, we loved reviewing your book and would love to publish it!"

Five years of writing and rewriting. Five rejections. But I only needed one acceptance.

Every time the manuscript was rejected, I was hurt and discouraged, but I knew that this book wasn't supposed to just be my own personal therapy session. I wasn't writing this book just for me. I knew that it was possible for me to get this published, and that's what kept me going; not vain pride that if I didn't become a published author I'd die a failure, but rather an unending drive to see if what I was really practicing was legit. Would believing that anything was possible for me, mixed with hard work and determination, help me reach my goal? Yes, it would, and it can help you reach yours too.

Remember: just because we've experienced something challenging doesn't mean that it's always been that way, and it doesn't mean it will continue to be that way forever. All it means is that we've experienced something difficult, and we can learn and grow and become better so that next time we'll be prepared to face it and beat it.

Here's a real-life example of how people believed that something was always going to remain the same and would never change—until someone proved them wrong.

In the 1950s there was a lot of hype around the sport of track and field. People were fascinated by other individuals' abilities to sprint at unbelievable speeds, jump at soaring heights, and stretch their bodies to the physical breaking point. There was, however, a universal belief among people that man was not capable of breaking the barrier of running a four-minute mile. Why? Because no one had ever done it. Sure, hundreds (possibly thousands) had tried, but no one (at least publicly), had succeeded in accomplishing this seemingly impossible feat—that is, until Roger Banister came onto the scene (Taylor, 2018).

In 1954, twenty-five-year-old Roger Bannister dispelled all the false beliefs that breaking the four-minute mile barrier was impossible. He clocked a 3 minute and 59.4 second mile time.

What happened after that?

Up until now, THOUSANDS more have done it, including high-school kids. What changed?

Did people suddenly develop stronger calves, thighs, hips, and cardiovascular endurance? Probably not. Were people waiting for someone else to do it first so that they didn't have "all the pressure" that comes from being the first one to do something? No.

What changed was the fact that because people saw someone else do it, their beliefs changed from "that's impossible" to "that's possible for me!" It had nothing to do with their physical stature. It had everything to do with what they thought was possible for them. What I'm saying to you is that if you know someone who has tried something that you want to try, or has done something you that want to do, or has become something that you want to become, then it's possible for you to try, do, and become that thing too.

What do you want to do? Chances are highly in your favor that someone else, since the earth was created, has done that thing.

Want to write a book? It's been done. Want to sing in a concert? It's been done. Want to cook a delicious French pasta dish with a delectable sauce? That's been done too.

"But Drew," someone may add, "it's different with those people. They were able to do it because they grew up in better circumstances than I did. They came from wealth and I came from dirt. They were so much smarter than me. It's unfair to say that 'anyone can do anything' when you don't actually know me personally."

You bring up a solid point there. Of course, we all have different physical, mental, and emotional limitations, but your future is not defined by your limitations, your circumstances, your parents, or your upbringing. It's defined by what you think is possible for you to accomplish; it's defined by YOU.

Do you think that Helen Keller had moments when she wanted to give up? Being blind and deaf, it would've been pretty easy for her to blame her circumstances for not producing much for her. But she didn't blame her circumstances. She worked hour after hour, day after day with her teachers and parents to develop a language and a vocabulary that she could understand and work with—and ended up earning multiple collegiate degrees and becoming one of the greatest inspirational minds of all time.

Another example is J. K. Rowling, the famous author of the *Harry Potter* series. Was she born into fabulous wealth, learning how to write soul-gripping fantasies from a young age? Not hardly. When she created the first book, she was an impoverished single mother living on welfare and fighting the dark clouds of depression. She was rejected several times when she pitched her first book, but eventually one publisher decided to take a risk on her—and the rest is history. She is the first official author to become a billionaire simply due to her novels (Giuliano, 2015).

What do Helen Keller and J. K. Rowling have in common?

Opportunity mixed with adversity.

That's what all of us have. We all have opportunities to prove ourselves, work hard, develop our skills, and believe that anything is possible for us to achieve. We also all have adversity. We have self-doubt, emotional, physical, or mental afflictions, or circumstances that are less than ideal. The key is to "play with the cards we are dealt" and figure out a way to make something out of nothing. That's the adventure of life, and it can turn into a glorious journey if we believe that it's possible for us.

You are blessed and highly favored! You have a lot going for you. You have good stuff in you, and it's possible that you can start to bring your passion and your creativity out into the universe.

I recently heard a story of two very good friends who both worked for the same corporation in Chicago. They had been loyal employees for more than twenty years, but during the 1980 financial crisis they were both laid off. For several weeks they both went out into the marketplace looking for a job, experiencing rejection after rejection. They would hear things like, "You're over-qualified," and "We can't afford to pay you a salary," and "We're not hiring at this time."

One of the men stopped. He became discouraged. He decided that it wasn't worth it to continue to put himself out there and try to find an opportunity to earn a steady income. As the days and weeks passed, he became very negative and argumentative with his wife, started drinking more and more alcohol, and would call his other negative unemployed friends every night and complain about how unfair his life was. He gave up.

The other man, however, continued to go out every day looking for work. He would start each morning reading the job section in the newspaper, would drop his resume off at different companies, and would seek referrals from past clients who knew him well. He faced rejection and discouragement, but he knew that if he didn't give up, *it was possible* for him to find work.

He finally went to a company and said, "Look, if you can't hire me at least give me some volunteer work. I'll do anything, and you don't have to pay me. I just want to be busy."

The employer agreed, and for the next month this individual was the hardest working person at the company. He was the first to show up and the last to leave. He would do things as menial as getting coffee for the CEO, to writing memos for various production meetings. Then, one day, after two months, one of the top managers quit.

Who do you think the company interviewed first for the open position? That's right—they interviewed the individual who didn't give up. They interviewed the individual who told himself every morning that it was possible for him to find work. They interviewed the individual who worked the hardest out of any full-time employee the company had. They interviewed and HIRED this individual (Brown, 1992).

What was the difference between these two individuals—the one who gave up and the one who persevered?

Eyesight and mindsight.

Eyesight operates out of our past and where we are now. If things have been going poorly or we haven't had much luck recently, eyesight will diagnose that as, "I can't do this. This isn't worth my time. I should just give up."

Mindsight, on the other hand, has to do with looking to the future with confidence and determination to make the most out of what comes our way. Mindsight will see a dire situation and say, "You know what, things haven't been going great, but that doesn't mean that things will stay that way. I have a lot of good things going for me. I can reach my goal. It's possible for me to achieve my dream. I am not going to give up."

To wrap things up, think back to that goal or dream you thought of at the beginning of the chapter. Envisioning it? Good. Now, are you viewing your goal through a mindset of eyesight or mindsight? Are you ready to give up because of setbacks and disappointments experienced? Are you tempted to throw in the towel and move onto something easier or less challenging?

Or are you looking at your goal through a different lens, a lens of possibility and hope? Are you looking at that thing you've always wanted to achieve and saying to yourself, "That's possible for me to accomplish! I can do that!"?

The choice is ours how we decide to move forward with our dreams. Now that we have this reminder that anything is possible for us to accomplish, it's our time to decide. Will we go for it, or not? Maybe some of us have realized that we spent too much time going for something and it wasn't even the right thing to go for in the first place. That's okay, too.

Don't just blindly follow what I said because you read it.

Be a student, not a follower. Decide what you want to do based off your own personal philosophy and experience, and then follow that path with all you got. And remember, no matter what you decide to go for, IT'S POSSIBLE for you to accomplish!

Chapter 8

GOAL-SETTING MADE SIMPLE

I know what you're thinking. "Great. Another chapter on goal-setting. I'm so sick and tired of being told what to do, and to be honest, goals turn me off. They make me feel so pressured to be perfect and to push myself harder than I actually can."

This is a legitimate thought, and one which I've had numerous people talk to me about. For some, goal-setting is just traumatizing. There's a lot of pressure to be perfect or to reach unreachable goals. For others, they feel like if they set a goal and hit it, they've somehow failed because they've been taught their whole lives that if you reach the goal you've set, then it was too easy to begin with. Still for some, they've had average experiences with goal-setting, but they don't quite understand the importance of it, or if it's worth it in the long run.

The point of this chapter isn't to "tell" you anything, or to "guilt-trip" or "scare" you into doing something that you feel uncomfortable with. My goal (see what I did there?) for this chapter is to help you understand the "why" behind goals and their importance, and to help you grasp the fact that goals aren't just for millionaires or professional athletes, they're for everybody at every stage of life—and they can be really simple.

DISCLAIMER: Before I write anything else in this chapter, I want you to know that there are many synonyms for the word "goal." I feel like a lot of people get turned off when they hear the word "goal" or the term "goal-setting" because they interpret it as some academic, soul-sucking idea, but really what we're talking about here is this:

goals are dreams. Goals are plans. Goals are nothing more than things you want to have, objectives you want to accomplish, places you want to visit, relationships you want to cultivate, or a fortune you want to obtain. So, as you read this chapter, remember that when I use the term "goal," you can substitute it with any of those synonyms I just described.

When I was young, my dad would always have us write down our goals once a year on December 31 so that we would have goals for the upcoming year. We would divide our goals into the following categories: physical, spiritual, academic, musical, and intellectual. I really had no idea what I was doing because I didn't know what a goal was or how it would help me, but I wrote down some random stuff so I could show my dad and go out and play with my friends. Years later, I look back and can uncover these two valuable lessons:

It's paramount that once we decide what our goals are, we write them down. A goal that isn't written down is simply a wish that can be forgotten or brushed aside in an instant.

Teaching kids how to set goals early in life is important, but what's more important is teaching them *why* you set a goal in the first place. If they don't understand the *why* behind goal-setting, it will just be another "thing they have to do" and won't benefit them very much.

Ask anyone who has ever achieved something of significance how they started, and I guarantee you that they will say they had a goal. Whether it's weight loss, increasing muscle strength, learning a musical instrument, starting at a new job, beginning a new relationship, or any other number of opportunities, they take a plan.

Why goals?

One of my favorite lines from Lewis Carroll's *Alice in Wonderland* comes when Alice is traveling down an unfamiliar road. You may remember that she comes to a crossroads with two paths before her, each stretching onward but in opposite directions. As she contemplates which way to turn, she is confronted by the Cheshire Cat, of whom Alice asks, "Which path shall I follow?"

The cat answers, "That depends where you want to go. If you do not know where you want to go, it doesn't matter which path you take" (Carroll, 1865).

Simply put, goals help us decide which path we will take in life.

Human beings are the only life-form on planet earth that can consciously change their life's direction whenever they wish. A dog can't be anything but a dog. A tree can't be anything but a tree. Human beings are immensely special in the way that we can live one way for five years, do some soul-searching and tear up that script, and then live a completely different way for the next five years.

Key phrase: we go the direction we face.

Another key phrase: we face the direction we design.

In other words, goals are like magnets, and the stronger the goal is, the stronger the pull will be in the direction we design.

Look at your life right now. Are you facing the direction you want to go? Have you designed a life that is yours, or are you simply living off borrowed time and ideas from someone else? Do you get up every morning motivated to run the day, or do you wake up in the morning with your fingers crossed, hoping that the day will run you? Any answer to these questions is fine, because after you read this chapter you will have the opportunity to decide if you want to continue on the path you've been trekking or if you want to change direction and follow a new path.

Now, someone may read this and immediately become discouraged because they've spent two, three, five, ten, or twenty years going in the wrong direction, and they feel like I'm shaming them or trying to make them feel like it's too late to change their lives.

NOT AT ALL.

Anyone who has ever lived on this planet can attest that direction determines destination, so it's paramount that we choose the right direction, or course correct when we've chosen the wrong direction.

If you've been on the wrong path for a long time, it's okay. The beautiful thing about life, and the most adventurous part about being a human being, is that we have the power to change our destination by changing our direction. If we don't like the way we are going, we can change it. If we don't like our current economic condition, we can change it. If we don't like our current address, we can change it. If whatever we're going through in life doesn't suit us, we can change it. If it doesn't please us, we can change it. If it doesn't make us happy or fulfilled, we can change it. We're not trees.

Here's a quick note to make: you cannot change destination overnight, but you can change direction.

If you've negatively messed around with your health for ten years, it'll take more than ten days to get it back—and the same goes for anything in life. If you've picked the wrong road and ended up in an undesigned destination, it'll take time to get to a newly designed destination.

But, here's the good news: it's only a small journey to get on the right road.

Most people think that in order to change their lives they need to change EVERYTHING, and that's a myth. All it takes is a little course correction. It starts with the simple things we learned as children. Mama said an apple a day keeps the doctor away. If you're not in the best shape of your life, then start by eating an apple a day; start by taking a walk around the block; start by drinking the water bottle instead of the soda bottle. You don't have to go to the gym for five hours a day. You don't have to start by eating only vegetables. Just start with the simple things.

Why is it so important to start with the simple things? Because one discipline adds to another. If you start with an apple a day, you'll start taking a walk around the block. If you start taking a walk around the block, you'll start going to bed earlier. If you start going to bed earlier, you'll start waking up earlier and taking advantage of the day. If you start taking advantage of the day, you'll start designing a life that is what you've always dreamed of instead of what someone else has planned for you—which isn't much.

The opposite is true as well. Lack of discipline adds up. If you choose the Hershey bar over the apple, you'll probably choose Netflix over the walk around the block. If you choose Netflix over the walk, you'll probably choose staying up late over going to bed early. If you choose to stay up late over going to bed early, you'll wake up late. If you choose to wake up late, you'll miss out on the opportunities of the day. If you miss out on the opportunities of the day long enough, you'll end up driving what you don't want to drive, living where you don't want to live, and ultimately becoming who you don't want to become.

It all starts with our goals and dreams, and the reason we have goals and dreams is they help us set the direction that we will follow in life, and the direction we follow in life will determine our destination in life. We don't set a goal to become a millionaire (substitute your own narrative) because of the money. We set the goal to become a millionaire because of what it will make of us in the process of trying to achieve it. Imagine the skills one must develop, the relationships one must cultivate, the character one must build up in order to achieve that status (not counting those who win the lottery, cheat their way to the top, or those who don't care about others in the process).

Reasons

Now that we have a little better understanding of the *why* behind goal-setting, let's talk about reasons. A reason is the glue that holds our goals and dreams together.

First off, it shouldn't shock you to know that everyone's reasons are different. Everyone sets goals for different reasons. For some, their reasons are personal; they like to set and achieve goals because it helps them feel good about themselves. For others, their reasons are based on their family; they like to set and achieve goals because it sets their family up for financial and relational stability. Still for others, their reasons are social; they like to set and achieve goals because when others see them succeed it gives them a rush of excitement and pleasure (thank you, social media). No reason is better than the other, and there are plenty of reasons out there, but understanding what your reasons are for doing something is key if you want to achieve your dreams.

Here it is: If you have enough reasons you can do anything.

Remember, reasons come first. Answers come second.

For example, you may know the name Andrew Carnegie. He was the wee little Scottish man who grew into one of the richest men to ever step foot in the steel industry. After he passed away some people were cleaning out his desk. In one of his drawers they pulled out a little piece of paper. On the back of it was Andrew Carnegie's life goal: "I want to spend the first half of my life accumulating wealth. I want to spend the second half of my life giving it all away" (Maxwell, 2014)

What a statement! What a goal! Andrew Carnegie is living proof that if you have a strong enough reason to succeed in life, then any obstacles or hurdles you experience along the way will only further your motivation to achieve.

Going back to Michael Phelps, why do you think he appeared in four separate Olympic competitions spanning over sixteen years? Was it because he felt obligated to go? Was it because his coach guilt-tripped him into over hundreds and hundreds of hours practice so he felt like he needed to compete? Was it because he had nothing better to do with his life, so he just swam and swam all day?

NO!

It was because of the joy! Because of the fulfillment! He so thoroughly enjoyed the constant satisfaction that came from setting and accomplishing such lofty goals that he was pulled to the Olympic games because that is where he could find out just how good he was—and having enough reasons to succeed is why he started in the first place.

Again, reasons come first. Answers (success, fulfillment, achievement, etc.) come second.

Stop reading. Put down the book. Take out a pencil and a sheet of paper, or your notes section on your phone, and think about what the reasons are for you wanting to achieve your dream. It doesn't matter what they are; just write them down. Write down as many reasons as you can until you feel so driven that you cannot live one more minute without going all out for what you want!

That's a Wrap

When it comes to making goals, don't put a limit on yourself. Make long-range and short-range goals. Dream for the future ten years ahead, and dream for tomorrow—and then write your goals down. Don't write your goals down based on what someone else expects of you. Write them down based on your own desires, passions, and ambitions. Don't overthink them. Most people think that a goal must be so "perfect" and "precise" that they get so overwhelmed before they even write the goal down.

Do you want to take your family to Europe next year? Do you want a new car? Do you want a new house? Do you want a new pair of shoes at the mall? Do you want to finish that book that you always get halfway through and stop? Do you want to save more money this month than you did last month? Do you want to become a more attractive person by exercising your mind and your spirit? Do you want to spend more time meditating and less time on Netflix?

All these examples are goals, and once you decide which ones you want to go for is when you can start to look at them more closely and see what it will take to reach them. What will the time line be? What skills will you need to develop? What money will you need to set aside? What will you need to stop doing, start doing, or continue doing?

Once you answer these questions, go for it! Go for your goal. Go for your dream. Put time and effort into reaching it. If you work hard, discipline yourself, and become something more in the pursuit of reaching for your goal, celebrate! Reward yourself for your grit. On the other hand, if you mess around, don't follow through, and miss the mark of your goal, feel the disappointment. Let that regret drive you to become something better.

Finally, when it comes to pursuing your hopes, wishes, dreams, and desires, be like a child. Why a child? Because children don't put limits on themselves. They dream of and imagine that they can do anything. Adults are too skeptical.

I once was sitting at a restaurant with my wife when a father and son sat at the table next to us. I didn't hear much of their conversation, but I did hear the child, who was probably ten years old, talk about his dream of playing in the National Basketball League (NBA). He wasn't saying, "If I play." He was saying, "When I get into the National Basketball League, I am going to make sure that you and Mom can come sit on the front row and watch me" (n.a., personal communication, 2020).

His goal was to make it to the NBA, and his reason for doing it was so that he could have his mom and dad come watch him on the front row. He didn't say how he was going to get there, or when, but his passion and faith in reaching for the stars was inspiring to me. It made me think over the next few days of these questions:

- Am I playing it too safe with my goals?
- Do I only set goals that are easy to reach because I'm afraid of failing?
- Do I need to add more childlike wonder and confidence to my goals?
- What can I do to have my goals be so inspiring that I can't wait to get up in the morning to achieve them?

I pose the same questions to you.

———— *Chapter 9* ————

WHAT FOUR YEARS OF BEING BULLIED TAUGHT ME

It was the BEST of times, and it was the WORST of times.

The Best of Times

I was born in Sandy, Utah, on January 25, 1996. When I was three years old, my dad received a job offer that would move us to New Canaan, Connecticut, on January 4, 2000. It was in this magical place filled with lush green trees, colonial homes, and an insane amount of humidity that I would spend the next eight years of my life. It was home. It was my childhood. I spent my afternoons with best friends swinging from branches in the woods behind my house, wading through the three-foot high river in front of my house, and playing hours and hours of baseball, basketball, football, wallball, soccer, and monopoly.

My best friend in the world was Tyler Edwards. He and I would spend almost every day together after school, and when it came time for the weekend, we would call each other's home phones (because texting didn't exist, and we were only nine years old) and ask if we could do a playdate. The next few hours would entail playing ghost in the graveyard outside, indoor basketball on his makeshift hoop with a "stop sign" as the backboard, and lots of Mario Kart DoubleDash on the then insanely popular GameCube.

I attended East Elementary School, where the theme was "Work Hard, Be Kind." I didn't really understand what it meant to be kind to others when I was that age. I guess I thought it meant "don't be mean to others" because it was easier to describe someone who was mean versus someone who was kind.

I loved my elementary school. My teachers, starting in kindergarten and moving up through fourth grade (because schools on the east coast graduate elementary classes after fourth grade) were Mrs. Dunn (a very kind old woman), Miss. Ellison (my first crush), Mrs. Callahan (who my good friend Austin Discala would call Mom on occasion . . . don't know why), Mrs. Michaelson (who taught me the importance of not lying to cover up another friend's mistakes), and Mr. Patrona (who could do the best Kermit the Frog impression).

It was at this school that I made some of the best friends of my life who I still talk to fifteen years later.

After fourth grade, my friends and I packed up our backpacks and moved to Saxe Middle School on South Avenue. I felt so mature and grown up being in the same school as eighth graders. It was at this school that I started to do "big kid" stuff like write three- to four-page research papers, participate in a reenactment of the Revolutionary War (I tried out for Patrick Henry but was offered a simple colonial citizen role instead), and made my first attempt at finding love (I approached this girl on the school bus and gave her a note that said, "I have a confession to make. I like you. I don't care if you tell your friends.") Yes, that is what I wrote word for word. Why do I remember it almost two decades later? Because it was that embarrassing and traumatic. Let's just say that girl didn't feel the same way, and I've never started another letter by proclaiming, "I have a confession to make," since.

Regardless of that last experience on the school bus, I loved my fifth and sixth grade years. Life was good. I had lots of friends, everybody wanted me on their sports team because of my speed, and it was always fun going into New York City once a month for a Broadway show or to visit Times Square.

Then, I turned twelve years old on January 25, 2008. Just two months after that I came home from school one day, and my mom asked me and my older brother to come into the living room. She had something to tell us. My dad was away on business, but he wanted my mom to deliver this exciting news.

"Boys," she said, "what do you think of this house?"

I didn't know what to think. My mom was looking at houses in Boulder, Colorado.

"I like it," I said. "Looks pretty big."

"Well," she added, "Dad got a new job offer, and we're going to move to Colorado at the beginning of May."

My brother and my jaws dropped. We were moving?! It took a few more days to wrap my head around the fact that I would be leaving my entire childhood, best friends, and amazing memories behind to venture out to a place I'd never been. But I quickly came to grips with it, and I couldn't wait to move to Colorado. But wait, it gets better.

Just three weeks later at the beginning of April, my dad was home and he called everybody into the family room. Turns out the company that offered him a job in Colorado got "outbid" by another company that wanted to give my dad a higher-paying salary in Utah!

"Matt and Andrew," he exclaimed, "we're moving to Utah instead! They need me there May 1, so we need to have everything packed and moved out by April 30."

"Wow!" I thought to myself. "I love Utah!" All my extended family lived in Utah. We would travel out there every summer to visit my grandparents, and it was where I was born. I was even more excited to move to Utah than I was to move to Colorado.

We landed at the Salt Lake City Airport on April 30, 2008—and our new adventure began.

In Utah, elementary schools go through sixth grade, so when I went to school the following morning it was interesting to go "back in time" to elementary school. But my class was awesome. Everyone in my class was so kind, and they all lined up to meet me after the morning bell rang. I immediately hit it off with a couple of those friends and would end up spending a lot of time with them, until the end of July.

The first week of August, my local scout group was going on a week-long camp out somewhere in Wyoming, and it was going to be an experience I would never forget. You see, when I was growing up I had very bad separation anxiety. It would come up at random times throughout my childhood and would last for an unknown period, but I'd always get over it. It was extremely difficult to cope with because one day I would be fine, and then the next day I would wake up and be in a constant state of homesickness, anxiety, and tears. It was very strange. It was after the very first night of scout camp that I woke up and experienced one of those "separation anxiety" times . . . and it wouldn't just last a week or a month—it lasted three years.

It was during this period of anxiety that I experienced the worst of times.

The Worst of Times

I don't know what it is about adolescence, but it seems that the main goal of every single boy and girl is to fit in—by whatever means necessary. This can inevitably lead to kids doing very stupid things, saying whatever needs to be said, and doing whatever needs to be done to come off like they are superior to those around them.

(Before I get going into this section, let me make one thing clear: this is not intended to be a pity party. The last thing I want anyone to think when they read this is, "Oh my gosh I feel so sorry for him . . . What a poor kid . . . What why didn't his parents do more?" I am sharing very sensitive and vulnerable experiences because I know that there are people reading this who have either gone through the same thing, or have kids, nieces and nephews, brothers and sisters, or other loved ones who are going through the same thing. I want those people to know that I understand them and I am here for them, and I want everyone else to know that bullying is real, that it's unjust and unfair, and that as we come together and make a stronger effort to be kind, we can one day overcome this problem.)

Because of my debilitating separation anxiety, my parents decided to homeschool me in seventh through ninth grade. That's right, the kid who grew up with so much confidence, was so outgoing, and planned on making more and more friends in Utah was going to be homeschooled for three years. Of course, at the time my parents didn't anticipate three years of homeschooling, but as my anxiety worsened and the bullying became more severe, they decided that would be best for me. From ages twelve to age sixteen I was bullied almost every day by the kids in my neighborhood.

I can still remember the first time I was called a retard by someone in my neighborhood. The kids in my scouting group and I were doing a service activity when suddenly three older boys ran up behind me, shoved me into the fence, and started to hit me in the private parts. When I told them to stop, thinking that a trusting adult was going to intervene (which they never did), they threw me on the ground and said, "You're such a retard!"

I got up off the ground, brushed myself off, and walked home with tears in my eyes. I had never been called a retard before. I thought kids were supposed to be nice to each other. I thought adults were supposed to watch out for those more insecure than them—especially children. I got home, slammed the door, and ran upstairs to my parents' bedroom to tell them what happened to me. They were just as shocked as I was, and exclaimed that I should "hit them back," and "call them a retard in return." To this day, I don't know why but I never wanted to retaliate. I never had it in me to call the bullies names in return, or to try and fight back. Maybe it's because I was short. Maybe it's because I wore glasses and I was afraid they would be broken. Maybe I just had a sensitive soul and didn't feel like stooping to the pitiful level of the bully would fulfill me or solve the problem.

Regardless, I would soon come to realize that this would be my life throughout all of middle school.

I couldn't go to church, scouts, or night games in the neighborhood without someone pushing me around, calling me "four eyes" (I've worn/ lost glasses since I was eighteen months old), telling me that I was such a baby for being homeschooled, teasing me because I didn't have as many friends as they did, or hitting me in the private parts.

It ruined the excitement I had of living in Utah. It heightened my anxiety. It started the hatred I would come to have of Utah for the following three years. It created a disgust for church and scouts and just playing outside. It lessened my self-esteem to the point where I would turn to pornography on an almost daily basis to try and numb the pain the bullies left in me. It grew my belief that my life would be terrible, and I would never have any friends ever again.

Trust me, when you're called a retard, and every synonym like it for three years straight, you start to believe that your future isn't worth being excited about.

It even got to the point where I would hide in my parents' car instead of going to church activities. I would tell my dad that I was leaving, get in the back seat of our 1999 Chevrolet Suburban, and hope that no one would come out to the car during that hour.

When I was sixteen years old, I was starting to experience cyber-bullying as well. Kids would text me crude messages, spread false rumors about me, or tell girls in the neighborhood that I was a weirdo and wanted to date all of them—creating friendship barriers that took months to break down.

I also remember when a group of my "friends" invited me out with them to ask girls to a dance. They all had girls to ask, and I didn't. They pressured me into asking this one girl that they knew didn't want to go with me but would be too nice to say no. They all got into my friends' car and made me drive by myself in my own car. As soon as I got out of my car to drop off the "invite" on her doorstep, they honked their horns and drove off, leaving me alone in an area that I had never been to before.

72

Now, some of you may be wondering, "Why didn't his parents do anything? Don't they love their son?"

First, thank you for the concern. My parents do love me very much, and they were just as heartbroken as I was about the bullying. But with all due respect toward them, I didn't take their advice. Their advice was to retaliate and fight back. Their advice was to suck it up and go to church, go to scouts, and go out and play in the neighborhood. I'm sure in their minds, through no fault of their own, they thought that it wasn't as bad as it seemed, and that because I already had anxiety, I was just blowing things out of proportion. Hey, I can't blame them. If I hadn't been going through it myself, I might have just told the kid to fight back and not to worry about it.

I don't blame my parents for anything that happened in middle school, and neither should you. What has been one of the major themes of this book? Taking responsibility for what happens to you in life and becoming better because of it, regardless of whether or not the fault is yours.

I was the one who decided not to fight back. I was the one who decided not to use mean words in return. It's true, I wished with all my heart that my parents would've just intervened and made the bullying stop. I wished with all my heart that they would've just come to scouts to see what was going on, But I am so grateful that they didn't.

Lessons Learned

Why? Because going through this four-year hell taught me a lesson I'll never forget and I'll never take for granted—it's called kindness.

Right after I got left behind asking that girl out to the dance, I found my way home, went upstairs into my bathroom, and said these words to myself. I remember them as clearly and vividly today as I did when I said them: "I will try to be kind to anyone and everyone I come across in my life. Why? Because I never want someone to feel the way I did."

Those words changed my life. Those words changed my perspective. Those words made the four years of bullying hell worth it.

If I had to go through that pain and that sorrow so that I would learn unequivocally that kindness was the way to a happy life, and that bullying was shallow and disgraceful, then it was worth it!

So, to those who you are reading this who have gone through past bullying experiences, or who are being bullied now, take heart in knowing that I understand your pain. I understand your sorrow. I understand why you don't want to go to school, or why you decided to start smoking or watching porn or doing stupid stuff with other kids who were also being bullied because you were trying to numb the pain. I get it. And just to clarify, I don't condone smoking, porn, or doing stupid things. I never said that. I said I "get it." I understand why someone would turn to those things. Are they healthy? No. Are they useful? No. Are they distractions from the real pain? Yes.

So, what can you do if you are being bullied, or know someone that is being bullied?

1. Hang in there. I don't know when the bullying will stop, or what the extent of it is, but I do know you're strong enough to make it through.

2. Everyone's circumstances are different. For me, not retaliating with physical or verbal force was right, but for you, it may be completely different. If you need to fight back to defend yourself or someone else, then fight. If you are more sensitive and don't have the desire to fight, or fighting would just make it worse, then stay calm and know that you are infinitely more than the bullies who are teasing you.

3. Don't give up hope for a happy life and kindness in the future.

4. Choose to be kind to everyone. Don't let the bullies make you lose your kindness.

   a. It may be the toughest thing to do in the moment, but looking back you'll understand that the bullies were the real cowards and you were the strong one.

   b. One of my favorite quotes is from Fred Rogers of *Mister Rogers' Neighborhood*. He said, "There are three ways to ultimate success: The first way is to be kind. The second way is to be kind. The third way is to be kind" (King, 2018).

5. Try and find activities that are productive and edifying when you're sad, such as:

   a. Reading a good book.

   b. Learning a new hobby or skill.

   c. Focusing on getting really good at a sport or excelling at your schoolwork.

As Frank Sinatra once said, "The best revenge is massive success" (Kaplan, 2012).

As hard as it may seem to persevere through the meanness and struggles you're experiencing, take those emotions and put them into becoming amazing at something. Go to the gym and work on your jump shot. Got to the rink and work on your skating. Go to the studio and work on your dance routine. Go into the kitchen and learn French cuisine. Take that pain and turn it into becoming the best version of yourself. I promise you, one day you'll look back at the life you've created, and you'll see the lives created of those who bullied you, and you'll finally understand why staying focused on being the best version of yourself, instead of getting even, was the absolute best thing you could've done.

Remember these two things:

First, some people would rather get even than get ahead. Stay focused on where you want to go.

Second, it's usually those people that no one imagines anything of who do the things no one can imagine.

Message to the Bullies

In conclusion, let me just say something to the bullies (as if I haven't thrown down on them enough in this chapter).

First, I think I know why you're bullying others. It's either because you're so insecure yourself that the only way you can feel better is to make someone feel worse, you're bigger/stronger than other kids and get a boost of dopamine by pushing them down, you are trying to "fit in" with a certain crowd so you try and show your dominance and power through making others feel small, you haven't yet discovered that the kids who are actually "cool" or "popular" don't break others down—they build others up, or because you think it's easier to be mean than it is to be nice and you've become used to that.

Key phrase: there is never a legitimate reason to be mean or to bully another human being. Ever.

I don't care if you're self-conscious about your weight. I don't care if you're self-conscious about your hair or your nails or your clothes. I don't care if you're new to the neighborhood and want to stand out. I don't care about any of those things. Bullying is never right, and you will always be the bigger coward when you're making others feel worse about themselves.

Now, if you don't like how someone is acting or living their lives and you think that bullying is the only way to get that person to change, remember these words that will forever be immortalized by Taylor Swift: "Shade never made anybody less gay" (Swift, 2019).

Just let that sentence sink in for a minute. Isn't it beautiful? Isn't it profound?

SHE IS 100 PERCENT RIGHT!

For some reason a lot of us think that if we're mean enough to someone or critique them just enough that they'll see their blind spots, change forever, and thank us endlessly for helping them improve. FALSE!

We can never influence lasting change in another human being through bullying, caddy remarks, physical abuse, sexual crudeness, or mindless manipulation.

If you really want someone to influence someone in a healthy way, make them feel better about themselves, not worse. Someone may change their behavior for a few days, a few weeks, or a few months because they're forced to, but the only way to change someone's nature is to lift them up and teach them to see their infinite value and destiny.

Stop being a bully. If you've been mean to someone, apologize. It can happen at school, in a marriage, in a family, in a workplace, and so on. Say sorry. Take responsibility for what you did and said. Don't make excuses or try and justify why you lashed out at that person. Decide to take the higher road, repair the emotional or physical damage, and choose kindness. And if you see someone else being bullied—stand up and speak out! Don't worry about what others will think of you. You'll never regret coming to the aid of someone who needs your help, regardless of how inconvenient it may be for you.

One Last Thing

To wrap things up, being kind to others is perhaps the noblest thing you can do in your life. It's not a weakness. It's not something you do only to the "cool kids" or those who you want to "like you." Be kind to everyone. Smile at everyone. Don't stoop to the level of the haters and those who are much more insecure than you. Live to see your life transform, your influence grow, and your happiness multiply.

---— *Chapter 10* ———

TWO DISCOVERIES TO MAKE IN LIFE

As you've most likely been able to tell throughout this book, the major factor in determining how your life turns out is you. Notice how I didn't say the "only" factor. Of course, there are outside circumstances, and even internal circumstances that can play key roles in our development. But for the most part, the *major* factor in determining if we win or lose in life comes down to one thing—ourselves.

There are two major discoveries that we can make to create the good life for ourselves and our loved ones. These aren't the only discoveries we can make, but they are essential for personal growth and fulfillment in life.

The first discovery we need to make in our lives is this:

It's not what happens to us that determines the quality of our destiny— it's what we do about it.

What happens to one of us happens to all of us. We all experience pain. We all experience loss. We all experience despair, discouragement, and despondence. These experiences are not saved for the liars, or the cheaters, or the saintly, or the honest. Life is no respecter of persons. As far as I can tell, we all agreed before we came to this planet that we would go through some difficult stuff, and it wouldn't matter if we were born in Kenya or Kentucky, into wealth or into obscurity, in two-parent households or an orphanage. We would all face challenges that would stretch us, hurt us, humble us, and provide us with the opportunity to either become better or become bitter.

All of us are in a little sailboat in life, and it's not the blowing of the wind that determines our destination. It's the set of the sail. The same wind blows on us all: disaster, opportunity, change, and so on. The difference in arrival is not the wind, it's the sail. And by understanding that life doesn't choose to "bully" one person and not another sets us up to become the best versions of ourselves.

You see, we can rip up the script that has been holding us back for the last five years and write a new script. We can take the awful things that have happened to us the last two months and turn those experiences into fuel for a better future. We can become agents of action instead of objects of inaction by acknowledging that when it comes down to where we end up in life, we are responsible.

We can't control what happens to us, but we can develop the skills, cultivate the wisdom, and build the character so that when bad times come, and they will, we have the strength and the fortitude to make it through stronger and better than ever before.

Here is an example of someone who started off with less than ideal circumstances but created a life that was far beyond what anyone ever thought or expected it would be. His name is Les Brown. He and his twin brother were born on a floor in an abandoned building in Miami, Florida, to a mother who gave them up for adoption. They were adopted by a single mother who worked as a cleaner for high-income families in their community. Each day she would clean for hours and hours, and at the end of the night the family would let her take leftovers from dinner home to her children.

Les wasn't always the smartest or most capable child. He found himself getting into trouble a lot while his mother was working. He was picked on by kids at school for being dumb and overweight. In elementary school he was held back a couple of grades and was "labeled" mentally retarded. Everyone around him considered him to have no future. He was clumsy. He was a slow learner. Others had put labels and expectations on him that created a paradigm of failure in his life. Sometimes his mother would take him to clean houses up in the wealthy neighborhoods in Miami, and he would tell his mother things like this:

"Mama, when I grow up, I'm going to earn enough money to buy you one of these houses."

"Mama, when I grow up, I am going to work so hard so that you don't have to come home at night and ice your ankles and your knees from scrubbing floors and dishes all day."

The kids at school would hear of his dreams and would tease him. No one like Les could do that, they thought.

Then, one day Les's life changed. He was in high school and was attending an after-school class with a friend. His friend was late, so the teacher, Leroy Washington, asked Les to go up to the board and write something.

Les said, "I can't do that, sir."

"Why not?" The teacher replied.

"Because I'm not a member of your class. I'm waiting for my friend."

"It doesn't matter," the teacher responded. "Go up to the board and write this down."

"I can't do that, sir," Les interjected.

"Well, why not?"

"Because I'm mentally retarded."

The teacher walked up to Les, grabbed him by the shirt (metaphorically), and said these words that forever altered the trajectory of his life: "Les, never say that again. Someone's opinion of you does not have to become your reality."

I'm going to repeat that one more time.

Someone's opinion of you does not have to become your reality.

It was in this moment when Les Brown realized that up to this point, he was being controlled by people's expectations and beliefs in him. He thought that life was intentionally picking on him for no reason.

Les decided from that moment on he was going to take full responsibility for his life—that regardless of what happened to him in the past, he was going to control his future. It didn't matter that he was born on a floor in an abandoned building. It didn't matter that kids at school teased him and teachers falsely labeled him. It didn't matter that he and his siblings slept on the floor in their home because it was so small. None of that mattered anymore. His future was up to him.

Les Brown used that fire to become the number-one motivational speaker in the world. In the past thirty years, he has spoken in hundreds of cities around the globe. He has written over a dozen books on becoming better, reaching goals, and making an impact. He has spoken for fees larger than $100,000 for an hour! He ran and was elected for public office in Ohio. He bought his mother the home he promised her he would. Ever since that day when he was a teenager with Mr. Washington, he has never let others' opinions of him become his reality (Brown, 2011).

Do what Les did. Take those experiences that have been gnawing at you. Take that pain from your past, or your present, that has been weighing you down and keeping you from being your best self and decide right here and right now that you're not going to let those things determine your destiny. It doesn't matter if you're in high school or in retirement. It's never too late to set a better sail and end up in a better destination.

The second discovery that we can make in order to create the good life for ourselves and those we care about is this: *Becoming the best version of ourselves is the most fulfilling way to get the most out of life.*

I don't know your pain. I don't know your sorrow. I don't know who has abused you or been unfair to you. I don't know the heartache that life has caused you up to this point in your journey. I don't know what addictions, illnesses, afflictions, or injuries you're experiencing right now.

But here's what I do know: the things that cause us the most pain, the things that try us the greatest, are stepping-stones needed to grow into the person we are meant to be.

As Steve Jobs once said, "You cannot connect the dots looking forward, you can only connect them looking backward" (Jobs, 2005).

It's extremely difficult to be our best selves when our bills aren't paid, our relationships are in shambles, our job is teetering on the edge of unemployment, our family situation is far from ideal, and so on. But what separates those who get the most out of life versus those who die with countless regrets is the ability to become the best version of themselves regardless of what is going on around them or happening to them.

Key phrase: the wealthiest place on earth isn't the bank, or the diamond mine, or the oil field. No. The wealthiest place on earth is the graveyard. Why? Because that is the place where so many inventions, so many books, so many businesses, so many relationships, and so many opportunities lie—dormant, dead, and irretrievable, never having come to fruition.

So, the question we must ask ourselves is this: what can we do in our lives *now* to make sure that by the time we go to our graves we go with minimal regret and maximum fulfillment?

May I suggest a few different ideas that will help us on our journey to becoming the best versions of ourselves.

First, understand the story of the golf ball. When the game of golf was first invented, those playing it hit a round, smooth, hardened ball with a club down a fairway. They hoped that their accuracy would point them toward the pin (goal), but what they noticed was that when they would hit the golf ball, no matter how accurate it seemed, the ball would sail to the left and to the right without exception.

As you can imagine, this was very frustrating for those who were doing a good job of hitting the ball. It just happened to be that they were playing with bad equipment.

So, someone went to work solving the problem.

After many "trial and error" scenarios, it was determined that the only way the golf ball would go toward the desired destination once it was hit (unless there was weather involved) was for it to have dimples or little dents all over it.

Now, what does that have to do with becoming the best versions of ourselves? We are a lot like the golf ball. We all start off as a smooth, round, and relatively plain looking object . . . and we all want to stay that way. We fully expect that by staying as this perfect object we will be able to reach our desired destination of wealth, health, happiness, and fulfillment. But then life shows up on our doorstep and tells us that's not how it works.

Life tells us that for us to travel the furthest toward our destination, we need to experience difficult things. We need to go through growing opportunities and moments of pain and fear. In other words, we need to have some dents on us. But, like the golf ball, we come to realize that the dents don't make us broken, they make us better. They give us just what we need to hit our goals, meet our expectations, and reach our destinations.

Second, the battle isn't in you external circumstances; the battle is in your mind. *It is not the movement of the clock that produces a newness of life—it's the movement of your mind.*

So many of us try to fix everything on the outside without first fixing what is on the inside, and I'm saying right now that if we can kill negativity in our heads, we can kill negativity in our lives. If you can control the thoughts in our heads, we can control the actions in our lives. As we talked about earlier in the book, all living starts with thought, and all thought results in who we become.

Thoughts lead to desires. Desires lead to actions. Actions lead to behaviors. Behaviors lead to who we become.

In other words, if we always do what we've always done, we'll always be what we've always been.

It's time to throw that old mindset behind us and embark on a new journey in life—a journey of first fixing what is in our heads, and then seeing what needs to be fixed around us; not the other way around.

(Again, I need to give a shoutout to those who experience mental/emotional illness. "Fixing" what is in your head is a process, and I am in no way downplaying your condition. I experience depression and anxiety on an almost daily basis. You do the best you can to be healthy and happy, and then see what the outside world needs).

We can decide right now that our lives will never be the same again. It doesn't take a new year, a different relationship, a new job, or a traumatic event for us to decide that a new mindset is needed. We can make it a reality whenever we wish.

As many of us can attest, just like new clothes don't make a new person, a new house doesn't make a new marriage. If you put the same old marriage in a new house, it won't make a difference because the same old problems will still manifest themselves.

A friend once asked me, "Drew, how can I attain an above-average salary? I feel like I'm just average in everything I do in life."

I responded, "Become an above-average person. Develop an above-average handshake. Cultivate an above-average smile, work ethic, and determination to succeed. Build up within yourself an above-average mindset" (A. Young, personal communication, 2020).

It's not hard to look around us and find someone or something negative. They're on social media. They're in our neighborhoods. Some may even be in our family. But we don't have to succumb to what is called stinkin' thinkin'. It can be so much easier to do the wrong thing than the right thing. It can be so much easier to give into negative or tawdry thoughts. But that's not how we grow. That's not how we create the good life.

We cannot step into our futures and still think in our pasts.

One will have to be left behind.

Lastly, in becoming the best versions of ourselves, we need to be aware of something: beware of what you become in pursuit of what you want.

Many desire to be the best versions of themselves "by any cost." They'll lie, steal, cheat, or even murder to acquire power and prestige. Little do they know, however, that one can only become the *best* version of themselves by staying virtuous, humble, faithful, meek, charitable, honest, and full of integrity.

We can't become the best versions of ourselves by demand or coercion. It's only when we understand that "it takes a village to raise a child" and it's all about values, virtues, and graces, that we truly become our best selves.

The story tells us that Judas got the money (see Matthew 26:14–16). Someone might think to themselves, "Well that's a success story, right? He got the money. Good for him."

It's true that thirty pieces of silver seems like a sizable portion of money in those days, but it's not a success story.

Why? His name was Judas! Doesn't that ring any bells? Judas, the traitor—the snake—the ex-disciple of Jesus Christ.

Well, the unenlightened person may respond to that, "I don't understand. If Judas had a fortune, why would he be unhappy?"

Answer: he wasn't unhappy with the money; he was unhappy with himself.

Key phrase: The greatest source of unhappiness is self-unhappiness.

In other words, those who look back on their lives and experience the agonizing pain of regret will experience it because of self-unhappiness. They will experience the sharp sting of remorse because they wasted too much time, they bullied too many people, they focused on accumulating dollar bills instead of healthy relationships, and they thought that holding grudges would be more effective in "sticking it to" their enemies than forgiving and moving on.

Life is too short to *not* work on becoming our best selves. Life is too short to be petty, hateful, and conniving. It may work for our benefit in the short term, but like Judas, we will all come to understand that life has an interesting way of responding to those who try and cheat it.

> I bargained with Life for a penny,
> And Life would pay no more,
> However I begged at evening
> When I counted my scanty store;
>
> For Life is a just employer,
> He gives you what you ask,
> But once you have set the wages,
> Why, you must bear the task.
>
> I worked for a menial's hire
> Only to learn, dismayed
> That any wage I had asked of Life
> Life would have paid (Rittenhouse, lines 1–12).

In conclusion, let us remember that life is the employer, and when we decide what we want and go for it, regardless of whether it is noble or wicked, life will reward us with an outcome that is suitable to our desires.

And just for your information, thirty pieces of silver in Christ's time comes to about two hundreds US dollars in today's world (Mullen, 2018). It was the price of a slave back then. Doesn't seem like much of a fortune now, does it?

So, let me leave you with this question: are you selling out yourself, your hopes, and your future for what seems to be a fortune but is really a fool's pay?

Remember: beware of what you become in pursuit of what you want.

Chapter 11

DON'T QUIT ON YOUR WORST DAY

Let me just say this before we go any further. I am not perfect at these things. I struggle with setting goals. I have a hard time controlling my thoughts. I wish I was a better and kinder person on occasion. That's life. We strive for the ideal while going through the refinement process of making mistakes, learning from them, and moving forward.

I've written this book because if applied, these lessons and principles can help all of us create a better life for ourselves and those we love. It's not meant to be a measuring stick for our imperfections. If I was perfect at all of these things in the book, I wouldn't have written it because I'd already be a millionaire living on a yacht in the Caribbean with my loved ones. Our whole lives are an opportunity to learn how to become better and go from grace to grace and skill to skill until we've reached our fullest potential.

Now, in the midst of reaching our fullest potential we come to understand one overarching fact about life—that it's HARD, UNFAIR, and UNPREDICTABLE. If you would've asked me when I was fifteen years old if I would've been suicidal at the age of nineteen, taking three different medications and going to counseling every two weeks, I would've laughed at you. There's no way I had the maturity or the foresight to even believe that would be possible .But life had other plans.

When we're striving to reach our goals, be better, and go for what is ours in the universe, we're going to experience some setbacks. Ever heard of Murphy's law? Simply put, Murphy's law states that anything that can go wrong will go wrong (as you can imagine, Murphy must not have been the most positive person to be around). We will all go through experiences that test us to our limits, that leave us reeling in fear on the floor of our closets or bedrooms, and that leave us exhausted, lonely, and defeated:

- The loan may not have gone through.
- You may not have been chosen for the part.
- Your business may have just failed.
- The diagnosis came back positive.
- The cancer has spread to multiple other locations in your body.
- Your mental and emotional collapses have left you depressed, suicidal, and discouraged.
- You've been let go from your job with two kids and a spouse to provide for and you feel hopeless.

It's called life!

Once we learn that it's not going to be easy (and remember that that doesn't mean it's always going to be hard either), we can start to not take things so personally. As we discussed earlier, life doesn't just go around looking for people to "bully." If it's our time to grow, life will come knocking on our door, and if we don't want to answer it, life will bulldoze them down, raid our fridges, and sit on our couches eating nachos until we've figured out that it doesn't move on until we learn the lesson we're supposed to learn in the particular circumstance we're facing.

So yes, life is hard—but it's not impossible. We can make it!

With new levels, come new devils.

I once learned a powerful life lesson from a lactation consultant my wife saw after our first daughter was born. What? Yes, you read that right. I learned one of life's greatest lessons from a lactation consultant.

When our daughter was born, my wife had the expectation that she would be able to breastfeed her. She had gone to various classes, had purchased various pumps, and thought that her body would naturally produce the milk the baby would need. A couple of days after our daughter's birth, my wife was noticing that her milk wasn't coming in. The baby would latch and try and suck for a few seconds but would start to cry because she wasn't getting any milk. We had numerous nurses coming into the post-partum room to coach my wife in different techniques and positions. We had lactation specialists bring in funny-looking gadgets and tubes to see if that would work. My wife was taking natural lactation pills to see if they would produce the desired result . . . and nothing worked. We left the hospital with a hope that Sabrina would produce but had a backup plan to use formula if she didn't.

After about two weeks of trying to pump twelve times a day, eating foods that would "promote better lactation," and using various nipple guards and feeding positions, my wife decided to go see a highly recommended lactation consultant. She just wasn't producing the milk she had always thought she would.

The consultant welcomed us into her office, and after about twenty minutes of more coaching and an attempt to feed our baby girl without success, she leaned back, looked at my wife, who was exhausted and defeated, and said, "You know what? You've been doing everything you can. You've been pumping, eating right, getting enough sleep, seeing specialists, and doing your best. I can tell that this just isn't working for you right now. You've had these grand expectations that you will be able to nurse your child and offer her your milk, but it's been harder than you thought. Let me offer you some advice: don't quit on your worst day."

That last sentence jumped out at me. No, I wasn't going through the pain of having to breastfeed our newborn child, but I was experiencing the pain of fatherhood, doubt, and exhaustion, and the unknown of what lay ahead. Both my wife and I were having a lot of "worst days." We both had numerous meltdowns, breakdowns, and days when we both wanted to quit. But those words rang true to me, and they rang true to my wife. We decided to give it one more shot, knowing that if biology was against us, we always had a backup plan and our child wouldn't starve.

It turned out that my wife couldn't breastfeed. She tried for another week and then stopped—and felt good about it.

What is the moral of this story?

We all are going to have hard days when all we want to do is give up. We all are going to have hours of loneliness, heartache, and turmoil. We all must go through "growing pains" in order to see how "tall" we can stand in life. Let the advice the lactation consultant gave my wife make a way into your life.

Don't quit on your worst day.

Keep going a little longer. Keep fighting a little harder. Keep striving a little more. Don't give up. Even if what you're going for now ends up not being the right thing for you in the long run, the only way you'll know for certain is by giving it one more shot. If it works out, great. If it doesn't work out, great! At least you'll know 100 percent, for who you become in the process of going for your dream is sometimes even more important than achieving it. The faith manifested, the courage captured, the hope instilled, and the discipline attained will all help as you continue down life's unpredictable roads.

The worst thing that can happen in our lives will not come from trying too hard. The worst thing that can happen in our lives will come from doing nothing at all.

If you haven't started, then start. If you've been paralyzed by fear, or procrastination, or uncertainty, just start walking, just start moving.

Good health starts with an apple a day. Good health starts with a walk around the block. Good health starts with reading a book instead of watching another episode on Netflix. Good health starts with a compliment instead of a criticism.

Good health starts with the little things and it ends with the little things. Don't quit on your worst day.

The Chinese Bamboo Tree

There's something in the far east called the Chinese bamboo tree. The Chinese bamboo tree takes five years to grow. It involves a very meticulous process of having to be watered and fertilized daily, and what's most interesting is that it doesn't break through the ground until the fifth year. But within five weeks of breaking through the ground, it grows ninety feet tall.

Now, the question must be asked: does it grow ninety feet in five weeks, or five years?

The answer is obvious—it takes five years for the growth to take place, because at any time if the watering, nurturing, or caring had been forgotten about or stopped, the tree would've died in the ground.

Can you imagine what people must've said to the caretaker who was nurturing the ground where the seed was growing those five years?

"Why do you keep watering that seed? There's nothing growing here."

"Why do you keep wasting your time? It's been two years and there's no tree."

"You know the tree already died in the ground. Otherwise it would've grown already. That's how trees work."

These questions won't be too different from the ones we'll be asked as we're working on growing ourselves as well.

"How long have you been working on your dream? Four years? And there's nothing to show for it!"

"Just give up already. If it was supposed to happen for you, don't you think you would've seen a result by now?"

"You know it only took me two months to reach my goal, so obviously you must be doing something wrong if it's taking you this long."

People are going to treat our dreams like the Chinese bamboo tree. They are going to diminish them, compare and contrast them, and even try to dissuade us from reaching for them. And some people, unfortunately, will stop working toward their goals. The results that they're searching for won't be immediate, so they'll try and find something more fleeting that will produce a desired outcome faster. They'll hear the voices of doubt and they'll start to internalize them. They'll start to care more about the opinions of their peers than the burning passion within their heart.

It's at this moment in time when we need to dig deep down within ourselves and proclaim, "You know what, I'm not where I want to be *yet*, but I'm a lot further along than I was before. It takes time to reach my goal. There's no such thing as an overnight success, and if I want to be the best version of myself, I need to put in the time and effort to nurture and care for my vision—no matter how long it takes. Come hell or high water I'm going after my destiny!"

The harder the battle, the sweeter the victory!

And you know what? Once we decide that nothing is going to stop us from becoming who we're meant to be (however long it takes), once we decide that our destinies are in our hands and no amount of persecution or pessimism is going to keep us from reaching higher—that's when we'll start to see results. And once the results begin to be attained, the loud cynical voices will start to become a lot quieter. They'll go from detracting to saying, "I knew you could do it all along."

But remember this: if they're not with you during life's thunderstorms, they don't deserve to be with you during life's sunshine.

Yes, growth is hard. Growth takes time. Growth takes commitment; and growth takes discipline. There will be days when we feel overcome with doubt, crushed, and devastated—like we're sinking in deep water with no lifeguard on duty.

But let me let you in on a little secret. *We might get knocked down, but we won't be knocked out.*

Conclusion

I would rather have us aim for the stars and not hit them than not aim for them at all.

I would rather have us go for it and not get it than not go for it at all.

Why? Because when we go for what is ours, when we strive to become all we can be, regardless of how long it takes or the hurdles we face along the way, we instill in ourselves the capacity to experience more joy and more happiness than we could've had we given only half-effort.

An oxymoron in life is that for us to more fully experience joy, we need to experience pain. For us to feel empathy, we need to feel humiliation, heartache, and sorrow. For us to feel happy, we need to feel sad.

And it's the same thing when it comes to creating the good life for ourselves and those we love. It takes time, patience, determination, endurance, pain, and discouragement. But be comforted: *nothing worthwhile in life comes with minimal effort.*

It takes someone anywhere between eleven and sixteen years post high-school education to become a practicing medical doctor.

It takes someone seven years post high-school education to become a lawyer.

Babies take nine months to develop and then another ten to fifteen years before they can start doing anything remotely resembling independence.

Creating great marital relationships take a lifetime.

Don't give up. Keep on going. It doesn't matter how many times you get knocked down. What matters is how many times keep getting back up and pushing forward.

> Good timber does not grow with ease:
> The stronger wind, the stronger trees;
> The further sky, the greater length;
> The more the storm, the more the strength.
> By sun and cold, by rain and snow,
> In trees and men good timbers grow (Malloch, lines 13–18).

You are enough.

You are worth the struggle.

You can make it.

Stand guard at the door of your mind and become the best you can be.

I believe in you!

WORKS CITED

Antanaityte, Neringa. "Neringa Antanaityte." *TLEX Institute*, 0AD, tlexinstitute.com/how-to-effortlessly-have-more-positive-thoughts/#:~:text=Tendencies%20of%20the%20mind&text=It%20was%20found%20that%20the,thoughts%20as%20the%20day%20before.

Aronson, Eric. "The Chinese Bamboo Tree." *Don Miller's Trading Journal*, 0AD, donmillerblog.com/the-chinese-bamboo-tree/.

Aurelius, Marcus. *Meditations*. Harper Press, 2020.

Bain, George Washington. *Wit, Humor, Reason, Rhetoric, Prose, Poetry, and Story Woven into Eight Popular Lectures*. Hardpress Publishing, 2012.

"BibleGateway." *Proverbs 29:18 KJV—Bible Gateway*, www.biblegateway.com/passage/?search=Proverbs%2B29%3A18&version=KJV.

Bombeck, Erma. "A Quote by Erma Bombeck." *Goodreads*, Goodreads, 0AD, www.goodreads.com/quotes/140315-worry-is-like-a-rocking-chair-it-gives-you-something.

Brown, Les. "It's Possible." *www.YouTube.com*, 1992, www.youtube.com/watch?v=TGA75TjcCfA&t=1818s, uploaded 2019.

Brown, Les. *Live Your Dreams*. Quill, 2001.

Carnegie, Dale. "Co-Operate with the Inevitable." *How to Stop Worrying and Start Living*, Simon and Schuster, 1948, p. 77.

Carnegie, Dale. *How to Win Friends and Influence People*. Simon & Schuster, 1936.

Carroll, Lewis. *Alice in Wonderland*. Macmillan, 1865.

Chapter 9: Matthew 26, www.churchofjesuschrist.org/study/manual/new-testament-student-manual/introduction-to-matthew/chapter-9?lang=eng.

Covey, Stephen R., et al. *The 7 Habits of Highly Effective People: Powerful Lessons in Personal Change*. Simon & Schuster, 2020.

Davis, Todd. *Get Better: 15 Proven Practices to Build Effective Relationships at Work*. Simon & Schuster, 2017.

Emerson, Ralph Waldo. "A Quote by Ralph Waldo Emerson." *Goodreads*, Goodreads, 0AD, www.goodreads.com/quotes/16878-do-not-go-where-the-path-may-lead-go-instead.

WORKS CITED

Emerson, Ralph Waldo. *Goodreads*, www.goodreads.com/quotes/51193-great-men-are-they-who-see-that-spiritual-is-stronger.

Giuliano, Karissa. "The World's First Billionaire Author Is Cashing In." *CNBC*, CNBC, 3 Aug. 2015, www.cnbc.com/2015/07/31/the-worlds-first-billionaire-author-is-cashing-in.html.

Groberg, John H. "What Is Your Mission?—John H Groberg." *BYU Speeches*, 4 Feb. 2020, speeches.byu.edu/talks/john-h-groberg/your-mission/.

Holland, Jeffrey R. "The Tongue of Angels." The Church of Jesus Christ of Latter-Day Saints, 2007, www.churchofjesuschrist.org/study/general-conference/2007/04/the-tongue-of-angels?lang=eng.

Jeffers, Susan J. *Feel the Fear and Do It Anyway: How to Turn Your Fear and Indecision into Confidence and Action*. Vermilion, 2007.

Johnson, James Weldon, and Rosamond Johnson. *Standing in the Need of Prayer: a Celebration of Black Prayer*. Free Press, 2003.

Kaplan, James. *Frank, the Voice:* Sphere, 2012.

King, Maxwell. *The Good Neighbor: The Life and Work of Fred Rogers*. Abrams Press, an Imprint of Harry N. Abrams, Inc., 2019.

Langbridge, Frederick. "Frederick Langbridge Quotes (Author of The Happiest Half-Hour, Talks)." *Goodreads*, Goodreads, 0AD, www.goodreads.com/author/quotes/3508961.Frederick_Langbridge.

"Live in Day-Tight Compartments.'" *How to Stop Worrying and Start Living*, by Dale Carnegie, Simon and Schuster, 1948, p. 7.

Malloch, Douglas. "Good Timber." *Poem: Good Timber*, Joseph Horn, 0AD, holyjoe.org/poetry/malloch.htm.

Maxwell, John C. *The 17 Indisputable Laws of Teamwork: Embrace Them and Empower Your Team*. Thomas Nelson, 2013.

Maxwell, John C. *Today Matters: 12 Daily Practices to Guarantee Tomorrow's Success*. Center Street, 2008.

Monson, Thomas S. "Follow the Prophets." The Church of Jesus Christ of Latter-Day Saints, 2015, www.churchofjesuschrist.org/study/ensign/2015/01/follow-the-prophets?lang=eng.

Mullen, Kathy. "How Much Were Judas Iscariot's 30 Pieces of Silver Worth?" *Grand Rapids Coins—Online Currency and Coin Dealer Grand Rapids*, 2018, www.grandrapidscoins.com/blogs/entry/how-much-were-judas-iscariot-s-30-pieces-of-silver-worth.

NA. "Owaves: Day in the Life: Michael Phelps." *Owaves.com*, 17 Aug. 2018, owaves.com/day-plans/day-life-michael-phelps/.

Nightingale, Earl. *The Strangest Secret; We Become What We Think About*. Nightingale-Conant Corp., 1957.

Pope, Alexander. *An Essay on Man. Epistle II*. Publisher Not Identified, 1733.

Rittenhouse, Jessie. "My Wage." *Poem: My Wage*, Joseph Horn, holyjoe.org/poetry/rittenhouse2.htm.

Rohn, E. James. *The Seasons of Life*. Jim Rohn International, 1981.

Rohn, Jim. "A Quote by Jim Rohn." *Goodreads*, Goodreads, 0AD, www.goodreads.com/quotes/209560-we-must-all-suffer-from-one-of-two-pains-the#:~:text=%E2%80%9CWe%20must%20all%20suffer%20from%20one%20of%20two%20pains%3A%20the,ounces%20while%20regret%20weighs%20tons.%E2%80%9D.

Rohn, Jim. "Rohn: 5 Simple Steps to Plan Your Dream Life." *SUCCESS*, 3 Jan. 2020, www.success.com/rohn-5-simple-steps-to-plan-your-dream-life/.

Scott, Richard G. "Using the Supernal Gift of Prayer." The Church of Jesus Christ of Latter-Day Saints, 2007, www.churchofjesuschrist.org/study/general-conference/2007/04/using-the-supernal-gift-of-prayer?lang=eng.

Stanford University. "Text of Steve Jobs' Commencement Address (2005)." *Stanford News*, 12 June 2017, news.stanford.edu/2005/06/14/jobs-061505/.

Taylor Swift. "You Need to Calm Down." *Lover*, 2019.

Taylor, Bill. "What Breaking the 4-Minute Mile Taught Us About the Limits of Conventional Thinking." *Harvard Business Review*, 10 Apr. 2018, hbr.org/2018/03/what-breaking-the-4-minute-mile-taught-us-about-the-limits-of-conventional-thinking.

Young, Whitney M. *Beyond Racism: Building an Open Society*. McGraw Hill, 1969.

Ziglar, Zig. *How to Get What You Want*. SIMON & SCHUSTER, 1978.

ABOUT THE AUTHOR

Drew Young is a native of the East Coast, growing up in Connecticut. He now resides in Utah with his wife and daughter.

Drew studied at Brigham Young University, where he was actively involved in teaching and developing curriculum for various student development courses. He's been sharing his story with numerous audiences around Salt Lake County for the past five years and has been featured in *LDS Living*'s YouTube series and magazine.

He serves as the publicity manager at FranklinCovey, where he assists in managing best-selling book launches and social media campaigns, as well as booking high-profile thought leaders, storytellers, and celebrities for On Leadership, the fastest growing and largest leadership development online newsletter in the world.

To contact Drew to speak at an event (or to just say "hello"), please visit his website at drewbyoung.com. He can also be reached at mrdrewbyoung (Instagram) and mrdrewbyoung1 (Facebook).